BELERION

ANCIENT SITES OF LAND'S END

BELERION

ANCIENT SITES OF LAND'S END

CRAIG WEATHERHILL

Bard *Delynyer Hendhyscans*
of the Gorsedd of Cornwall

ALISON HODGE

First published in 1981 by Alison Hodge, Bosulval,
Newmill, Penzance, Cornwall TR20 8XA.

© Craig Weatherhill, 1981.
Reprinted 1985, 1989.

ISBN 0 906720 01 X

Designer Stuart Hamilton

Typesetting and origination by TNR Productions Ltd,
19 Westbourne Road, London N7.

Printed and bound BPCC Wheatons Ltd., Exeter.

DEDICATION

*For Vivien Russell and Peter Pool, without whose friendship and
guidance this book could not have been written.*

ACKNOWLEDGEMENTS

A book such as this cannot be produced without a great deal of help
from others, and I should like to express my sincere thanks to the
many people and organisations who have encouraged and assisted
me, especially Mr. and Mrs. Peter Pool, whose friendship and
guidance have been invaluable; Vivien Russell, whose years of work
inspired me; Peter Marshall for taking and processing many of the
photographs, and for his willingness to help; RNAS Culdrose for
allowing me to reproduce the aerial photographs; the Cornwall
Archaeology Unit and the Royal Institution of Cornwall, for allowing
full access to their records; the Cornwall Archaeological Society; Alison
Hodge for giving my work a chance; and the native population of West
Penwith, who are among the most genuine folk on earth.

Craig Weatherhill
Falmouth, 1981

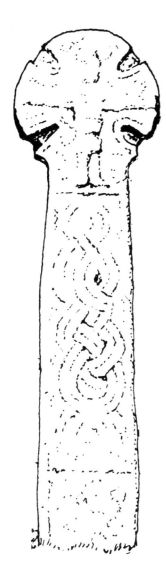

CONTENTS

Introduction

The Land's End peninsula, or West Penwith, the Belerion of classical writers, is a must for anyone with an interest in the past, whether they be professional archaeologists and historians or casual visitors with an eye for the ancient. It is a living museum: within its 87 square miles there are around 800 known and visible archaeological sites; and a further 400 or so are known to have existed. This is a greater concentration of ancient sites than almost anywhere else in Britain.

West Penwith is a bulky, granite peninsula separated from the rest of Cornwall by a low-lying isthmus only four miles wide, across which the Hayle River runs. West of this, the land rises rapidly into a succession of high, bleak moorland hills, rich in tin and copper and a major centre of prehistoric culture. The range of granite hills, many of them topped by a 'carn' or tor, runs in a rough line from south-west to north-east, occupying an area 11 miles long by 3½ miles wide. The highest points, all close to the north coast, are the hills of Watch Croft, or Morvah Hill (826ft/252m), Trendrine Hill, also known as Merra or Wicca Hill (812ft/248m), and Carn Galva —spelt Galver on recent Ordnance Survey maps — (800ft/ 244m). These hills are surrounded by a coastal shelf, incised by valleys, which is about 300 to 400ft (91 to 122m) above sea level. On the north coast, this shelf has an average width of only half a mile, but on the south, below a line drawn between Land's End and Penzance, it bulges to around three miles wide. This coastal shelf supports the majority of the present day farmland. The coast is notoriously savage and spectacular, with cliffs from 200ft (61m) to 400ft (122m) high, and nowhere in West Penwith is it possible to be more than three and a half miles from the sea. Its scenery and archaeology are major reasons why most of the Land's End peninsula has been officially designated as an 'area of outstanding natural beauty, great scientific and historic value'.

The position of West Penwith, jutting out into the ancient sea-route along the Atlantic coasts of Europe, and its mineral wealth were major factors in its prehistoric importance, for its people supplied tin to much of the western world for the manufacture of bronze. It was the first place in Britain to be described in documentary record, following the visit of the geographer Pytheas of Massilia (Marseilles), c. 325 BC, whose observations formed the basis of works by scholars like Diodorus Siculus of the first century BC. An important extract from Diodorus is included in the introduction to the Iron Age section of this book.

The majority of Penwith's ancient monuments are on the high moors, probably because there they have been spared from the ravages of agriculture, but a number do still exist on the lower land. Due to their isolation, most of these sites, often in magnificent condition, are little known, the exceptions being the nationally famous Lanyon Quoit, the Mên-an-tol and the Iron Age village of Chysauster. Very few of them have had plans of any detail published before, but the author is steadily surveying all the existing sites so that records in plan form will at last be available. Many of the plans in this book are based on these surveys. Only a handful of sites have been extensively excavated, but the condition of many of those which have not is astonishingly good.

Some of West Penwith's monuments have a link with the present; for instance the Iron Age hill fort of Lescudjack Castle may well have been the origin of Penzance, now the 'capital' of the Land's End peninsula. Many more are linked with legend which, in some cases, may give clues to the origin and purpose of a site. Brief accounts of these legends are given with the descriptions of the sites.

A hundred of Penwith's finest monuments are described in this book, which is divided into four sections:
1) Sites of the neolithic era (4300 – 2100 BC)
2) Beaker period and Bronze Age sites (2400 – 800 BC)
3) Iron Age sites (800 BC – AD 410)
4) Sites of the Dark Age and Early Christian period (AD 410 – AD 1066).

The last section also includes some notable post-Norman sites which, although late in date, cannot be excluded.

For the adventurous, there are two walks along Penwith's major prehistoric trackways, for this is a marvellous way of visiting a large number of ancient sites and experiencing the unique, some say weird, atmosphere of the spectacular Penwith moors, described by C.E. Vulliamy as 'what is most beautiful and unknown in Cornwall.'

A living, yet ancient, monument is all around you in West

Penwith, in the form of place-names derived from the Cornish language, a Celtic tongue of the Brythonic group which includes Welsh and Breton, the latter being closely akin to Cornish. Pronunciation of these names is always a difficulty for the visitor and a list of place-names, with their derivations and pronunciations, is to be found at the end of the book with a list of the mysterious Land's End saints – in reality Celtic Christian missionaries of the fifth to seventh centuries AD.

A map is always necessary when exploring any area and the most popular map covering West Penwith is the Ordnance Survey 1:50,000 sheet 203, *Land's End and the Lizard*, which recently superceded the one inch scale maps. This map should be used in conjunction with this book, which gives the National Grid reference (NG) of each site, and how the site is marked on the map. The National Grid system of location is explained on each Ordnance Survey map. For greater detail, the 1:25,000, or 2½ inch Ordnance Survey sheets SW 32/42, SW 33, SW 43 and SW 53 cover most of the Penwith area. The National Grid system also applies to these maps.

The abbreviations NT and DE will be found in the book. These indicate monuments which are under the guardianship of either the National Trust or the Department of the Environment.

Seekers of Penwith's Past

In 1700 AD, plans of one of two local sites – notably Chûn Castle and the Boskednan stone circle – were produced by Edward Lhuyd, and about the same time Thomas Tonkin made drawings of the now totally destroyed courtyard house village at Higher Bodinnar, near Newbridge. These remained unpublished until very recently, but they did mark the beginning of the archaeological study of the Land's End peninsula.

The true 'father of Cornish archaeology' was Dr William Borlase (1696-1772) who, for fifty years, was rector of Ludgvan. Born at Pendeen Manor, his childhood interest was probably aroused by exploring the Iron Age fogou known as Pendeen Vau, which happened to be in his back garden. His study of Cornish antiquities resulted in his magnificent work, *The Antiquities and Natural History of the County of Cornwall*, published in 1754. Although he tended mistakenly to credit the druids with a number of ancient sites – most much earlier than druidism – and even with

some natural features, his work continues to be of great value.

In the nineteenth century, Dr Borlase's work was continued by two outstanding archaeologists. One was his descendant William Copeland Borlase (1848-99), who conducted a number of excavations, reports of which were largely published in his *Naenia Cornubiae* (1872). The other was John Thomas Blight (1835-1911), a man of equal gifts whose career was tragically cut short by a mental breakdown which confined him to an asylum for more than half his lifetime.

In the twentieth century, many people have come to the fore, some of whom should have a special mention. Lieut.-Col. F.C. Hirst founded the West Cornwall Field Club in 1935 and was the first to recognise and study the important Iron Age dwelling type now known as the courtyard house. Charles Henderson, who died in 1933, at the early age of thirty-three, left valuable and lengthy records of many sites in West Penwith and throughout Cornwall. Professor Charles Thomas, now director of the Institute of Cornish Studies, also has a long and distinguished archaeological record, as has Mr Peter Pool of Penzance, a major contributor to our knowledge of Cornwall's past. Miss Vivien Russell must never be omitted from such a list; her *West Penwith Survey* (1971), cataloguing all known archaeological sites of the locality, whether existing or destroyed, represents over thirty years of painstaking and dedicated work.

Even after nearly 300 years, the study of West Penwith's long and distinguished past is still only in its youth. Today, when interest in archaeology is increasing at an astonishing rate, the author is just one of a rising generation of young archaeologists, and the setting up of a guardian body, the Cornwall Committee for Rescue Archaeology (under the expert eye of Professor Thomas), has been a great asset to all concerned with the recording and preservation of Cornwall's ancient heritage.

The Cornwall Archaeological Society, which grew out of Lieut.-Col. Hirst's West Cornwall Field Club, is a fine movement with an ever-increasing membership and produces an excellent annual journal, *Cornish Archaeology*.

Other stalwart bodies concerned with Cornwall's past are the Federation of Old Cornwall Societies and the Royal Institution of Cornwall, which is based at the County Museum, Truro. This museum must not be missed, and among others which should be visited are the Penlee Museum in Morrab Road, Penzance and the fascinating little Wayside Museum at Zennor.

Archaeology and the Law

All the sites described in this book are Scheduled Ancient Monuments and, as such, are protected by law. Excavations, however small, must be carried out only by *qualified* archaeologists, and then only with the sanction of the Department of the Environment. Unauthorised, unqualified excavation, and damage of any sort to ancient monuments is strictly illegal and carries severe penalties. Metal detectors are the latest menace to our ancient heritage, and while most users of these instruments act with admirable conduct, much damage may be caused by the irresponsible few. (In any case, metal objects, especially those made of ferrous metal, do not easily survive in Cornwall's acid soil.) Should you be a witness to damage of an ancient monument, do not hesitate to inform the Cornwall Archaeology Unit (telephone Truro [0872] 74282, extn 3603).

As many sites are on farmland, the country code also needs a mention. The average Cornish farmer is friendly and helpful; but not if his gates are left open, if dogs are let loose among his livestock, if litter is left on his land or if his crops are trampled. If no footpath exists, keep to the very edges of fields and always ask the farmer's permission to cross his land. His hospitality is both generous and genuine. Please don't abuse it.

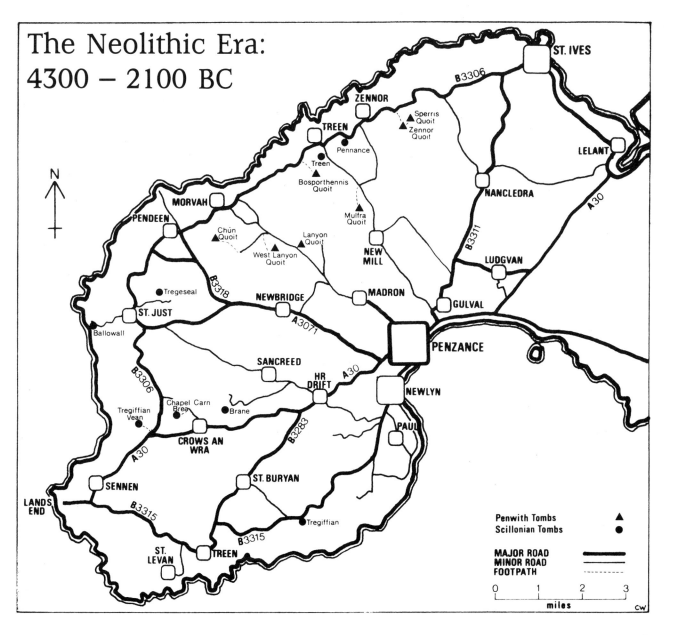

The Neolithic Era: 4300 – 2100 BC

N

ST. IVES

B3306

ZENNOR

TREEN

Sperris Quoit ▲
Zennor Quoit ▲

LELANT

Pennance ●

A30

Treen ●

NANCLEDRA

Bosporthennis Quoit ▲

B3311

MORVAH

Mulfra Quoit ▲

PENDEEN

Chûn Quoit ▲

Lanyon Quoit ▲

NEW MILL

West Lanyon Quoit

LUDGVAN

Tregeseal ●

B3318

NEWBRIDGE

MADRON

GULVAL

ST. JUST

A3071

Ballowall ●

PENZANCE

B3306

SANCREED

HR DRIFT

A30

NEWLYN

Chapel Carn Brea ●

Brane ●

PAUL

Tregiffian Vean ●

B3283

A30

CROWS AN WRA

ST. BURYAN

SENNEN

Penwith Tombs ▲

LANDS END

B3315

Tregiffian ●

Scillonian Tombs ●

B3315

MAJOR ROAD
MINOR ROAD
FOOTPATH

ST. LEVAN

TREEN

0   1   2   3
miles

CW

The Land's End peninsula seen by the first neolithic settlers more than 6,000 years ago was not vastly different from the place we see today. The bare, windswept moorland heights are still more or less as they were then, but the valleys and sheltered parts of the lower ground were thickly wooded. To their gaze, St. Michael's Mount would have been a gaunt outcrop rising from a dense, low-lying alder forest threatened by every spring tide. It was not until about 2000 BC that the Mount's Bay forest was finally inundated, turning the Mount into the island it is today.

These small, adventurous people were Britain's first farmers and, by clearing areas of woodland and cultivating the ground, were the first men to alter the face of the British landscape. Why they came at all is somewhat of a mystery – perhaps rumours had spread of this fertile island on the northern edge of their known world. But come they did, ferrying their grain and their livestock across the Channel in small boats of wood and hide. The little groups that arrived on the shores of Britain did not find an altogether empty land: man had been in Britain for at least a quarter of a million years. Before the sea broke through to form the English Channel, c. 8000 BC, it was possible to walk over from the Continent.

These earlier people were few and far between, but the neolithic farmers found the remnants of palaeolithic (old Stone Age) men and the tall, dark mesolithic (middle Stone Age) people, both of whom were nomadic hunters, fishermen and flint-workers, and neither of whom left any visible monuments of their time. The new arrivals met no resistance or aggravation; there was more than enough room for everyone. Agriculture had been born long before in the Near and Middle East and its knowledge slowly spread through the western world. By 4000 BC, the neolithic (new Stone Age) settlers had brought it to Britain.

They seem to have been an attractive people, averaging 5ft 4ins (1.6m) in height, with a slender, athletic build. Their long hands and skulls conjure up a picture of sensitive, delicate features. It is thought that they were predominantly dark-haired. Legend may possibly give us an insight into their ways of life. An ancient local tale of the Small People, which may well be folk memories of the neolithic people, stated that they were star-worshippers and that they had no such thing as marriage. If a child was born, any one of the menfolk could have been the father and great celebrations were held. That this is a glimpse of neolithic life is only a possibility, but nonetheless a fascinating one.

Neolithic settlements were of both permanent and temporary types. Their primitive farming methods tended to exhaust the soil and, when this occurred, they would move on to start another farm. As yet, no neolithic settlements have been identified in West Penwith, but various finds show that a number of these people did live and work in the peninsula. One of many probable dwelling sites was on Trencrom Hill near Lelant where a pair of neolithic axes was found on the hillside. However, the only visible and known archaeological remains on the hill are Iron Age.

The nearest known neolithic settlement to the Land's End peninsula was found a few years ago on Carn Brea, the monument- and castle-crowned hill above Redruth and Pool, somewhat to the east of our area. Excavations of the giant Iron Age complex on the hilltop revealed that in one place it overlaid a stone-walled settlement of neolithic date, one of the oldest known villages in Britain.

Pottery of this period dates from as far back as 4000 BC and is of a distinctive type which was found in quantity at a neolithic site in Wiltshire. The first neolithic culture takes its name from this site: the Windmill Hill people.

Flint sources are known in the area. This versatile stone was used to make polished axes, arrowheads with a distinctive leaf shape, scrapers for cleaning skins and various other kinds of blade. One source of trade which grew rapidly during the neolithic era was the manufacture and distribution of stone axes. Made of granite and greenstone, and often highly polished, Cornish-made axes have been found all over Britain, and at least four sources of these were in West Penwith: near St. Ives, the area of Land's End itself, Kenidjack Castle near St. Just and the Gear Rock just off Penzance. Now surrounded by the sea at all tides, this last site was then on dry land.

By 2500 BC, a number of secondary groups of neolithic settlers were arriving, and trade routes were coming into being. Many of these ancient tracks, or ridgeways, which continued in use for thousands of years, are still in existence. West Penwith had its own system of trackways, and the most important of these will be described in more detail later in this book.

Around 3000 BC, a new race of people arrived, having spread through the Mediterranean countries and western Europe. These were the megalith builders, the designers, builders and engineers of the extraordinary great stone tombs which are such an awesome sight today. (The word 'megalith' derives from the Greek for 'great stone'.) In West Penwith, they appear to have arrived in two separate waves. The first were the builders of a specialised type of mass tomb known locally as 'quoits', and more officially as *Penwith chamber tombs*. Although these are found elsewhere in Cornwall, the major concentration is in the Penwith peninsula, hence the name. These, the oldest of all remaining Cornish structures, consist of a number of great upright slabs forming a burial chamber which was roofed by a huge, single capstone many tons in weight. They were probably in use for several hundred years; as a chieftain died, so his body was placed with those of his predecessors. (It has to be said, though, that very few human remains have been found in the Penwith tombs, probably due to grave-robbing in antiquity.) These 'quoits' were finally covered by great mounds, or 'barrows' of earth and stone. At many sites the remains of the mound are still visible although wind, weather and, most of all, man, have worn them all down, revealing the skeletal stone chambers beneath.

The second wave of megalith builders, which appears to have developed in the region of Finisterre, in north-western Spain, produced a peculiar type of megalithic tomb which is to be found only in the Isles of Scilly and West Penwith. The islands seem to be covered with them, hence the name *Scillonian chamber tombs*, or more popularly 'entrance graves'. A Scillonian chamber tomb consists of a passage-like stone chamber roofed by a number of slabs, and usually opens at one end onto the outside of the earth and stone mound covering it. This mound is often retained by a 'kerb' of large stone blocks. Like the quoits, the use of entrance graves continued for many centuries, and a few finds of middle and even late Bronze Age pottery suggest re-use of the tombs and perhaps a lingering of the megalithic culture.

Other types of neolithic monument, 'causewayed camps' and 'henges' for instance, are not definitely known in West Penwith although there has been some suspicion about two sites. The Iron Age hill fort of Caer Brân *(Site 48)* was thought by some to have been built on the site of a causewayed camp. This is doubtful, but should it prove to be so, it would be the only one in Cornwall. As for henges, three do still exist in Cornwall, but none are in west Cornwall. These presumably ritual earthworks consists of a bank and internal ditch surrounding a flat central area which sometimes carried a stone or timber circle. They were invariably sited close to ancient trackways and so is the curious Treen Common circle *(Site 34)* which may represent a type of henge but, again, there is much doubt as to what this site really was.

Fifteen established sites of the neolithic era are well-worth visiting in West Penwith, all of them tombs of either the Penwith or Scillonian type. They are listed below.

1 The Ballowall Barrow, Scillonian Chamber Tomb, St. Just. DE.

NG 356312. *Marked as:* **Chambered Cairn.**
1 mile W of St. Just, taking lane marked 'Carn Gloose'. Barrow stands by roadside on clifftop.

A huge, complex and magnificent monument consisting of a large, closed chamber within a central dome; this being surrounded by a later collar or cairn-ring. The whole structure, the like of which is unknown, is built of stone. The central chamber contained a number of stone cists (small slab coffins) which have now gone, and a curious T-shaped ritual pit which can still be seen. The central dome, slightly oval and with a larger diameter of 37ft (11.2m), has lost its top but still survives to a height of 10ft (3.0m).

Two cists can be seen in the narrow space between the corbelled dome and the collar,

which is slightly later in date. This contains a smaller recess which also has a pit cut into its floor. Opening onto the outside of the collar, which is some 20ft (6.1m) thick and as much as 8ft (2.4m) high, is a well-preserved entrance grave 11ft (3.3m) long and 3ft (0.9m) high, roofed by two thin slabs.

Excavations by W.C. Borlase in 1878-9 revealed that the cists contained urns and cremated bones of the middle Bronze Age, perhaps a hint that this astonishing mass tomb was built by people who preserved the megalithic culture for many centuries and against all odds.

Legend speaks of the Small People who are said to dance around the great barrow on moonlit night; a folk memory, perhaps, of sacred rituals that were once performed by the last of the megalith builders.

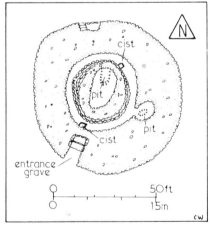

Ballowall Barrow (1)

2 Bosporthennis Quoit, Penwith Chamber Tomb, Treen (North).

NG 436365. *Not marked.*
Footpath S from B3306 at foot of shallow valley just W of Porthmeor Farm. After about 300m, cross to W side of stream. The Quoit lies in a small field just S of this point.

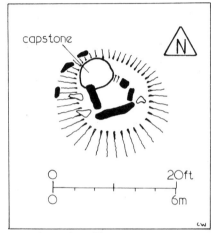

Bosporthennis Quoit (2)

The Quoit, located in a field bounded by massive walling, is still firmly embedded in an oval barrow about 20ft (6.1m) across and 2½ft (0.8m) high.

The chamber retains three of its four sides formed by upright stones, one of which is 5ft (1.5m) high. The enclosed area measures 5ft by 4½ft (1.3m). The dismounted capstone is unusually thin and is of a curious oval shape with a greater diameter of 5½ft (1.6m). It is said that a local miller was responsible for trimming it to its present shape before deciding that it was unsuitable for a millstone.

W.C. Borlase excavated the tomb in 1872, finding sherds of pottery and calcined bones. Its small size makes it difficult to classify, being somewhere between the sizes of the average Penwith tomb and the average cist.

3 The Brane Barrow, Scillonian Chamber Tomb, Sancreed.

NG 401282. *Marked as:* **chambered barrow.**
3 fields SW of Brane Farm (see Carn Euny Iron Age courtyard house village, Site 50, for directions).

Also known as the Chapel Euny barrow, this entrance grave is perhaps the best preserved example of its type in West Penwith with its passage and kerbed mound intact. The mound is 20ft (6.1m) in diameter and 7ft (2.1m) high.

The chamber, which opens onto the south-eastern side of the barrow, is 7½ft (2.3m) long, 4ft (1.2m) wide and 3ft (0.9m) high. It is roofed by two stone slabs. The surrounding kerb is unusually heavy for a tomb of this size.

The barrow owes its preservation through the last two centuries to the fact that for some time it was regarded as a convenient sheep shelter.

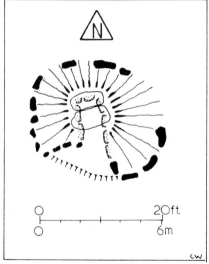

Brane Barrow (3)

4 Chapel Carn Brea, Scillonian Chamber Tomb, Crows-an-wra. NT.

NG 386281. *Marked as:* **tumulus.**
Minor road linking A30 to B3306 leads NW from the hamlet of Crows-an-wra. Footpath on left ½ mile from this junction leads to hilltop.

The first barrow on the top of the 'First and Last' hill was an entrance grave 30ft (9.1m) across holding a chamber 9ft (2.7m) long, with a curiously tapered inner end. This, however, was just the beginning of a fascinating history. During the early Bronze Age, a burial cist was set on the side of the barrow and the whole site was buried beneath another stone mound. At a later stage, the cairn was enlarged yet again, the result being an immense sugar-loaf shaped pile 15ft (4.6m) in height and 62ft (19m) across, with an outer kerb and no less than three internal and concentric retaining walls. Objects found within this massive cairn date from the late neolithic (at the bottom) to as late as the Dark Age (AD 410 to AD 1066) in the upper layers.

In the thirteenth century, the tiny hermitage chapel of St. Michael of Brea was built on the very top of the cairn. Here the hermits kept a beacon for the guidance of local fishermen and for land-travellers (a major ancient trackway passes the hill). The chapel was demolished in 1816, having become a dangerous ruin, and its stone was used to build a barn at the foot of the hill.

During World War II, the hill was occupied by the military for use as a radar observation post. They built their radar post on the cairn itself, destroying the work of 4,000 years ago. Now all that is left is a shapeless pile of stone 9ft (2.7m) high. Two of the inner retaining walls are partially exposed and the secondary stone cist, complete with heavy capstone, is also in full view on the south side. It is not known whether the original entrance grave is still buried beneath the mound or whether it has been destroyed.

Chapel Carn Brea was the site of at least eight barrows and seems to have been of some funerary importance. The hill has long been the

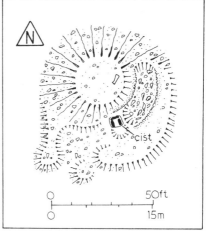

Above & below: *Chapel Carn Brea (4)*

site of both traditional midsummer bonfires and alarm beacons and the former are still lit there, with full ceremony spoken in Cornish, each midsummer's eve.

9

5 Chûn Quoit, Penwith Chamber Tomb, Morvah.

NG 402340. *Marked as:* **Chûn Quoit.**
Just W of, and visible from the Iron Age fort of Chûn Castle (see Site 54 for directions).

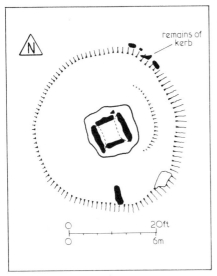

Above & below left: *Chûn Quoit (5)*

This magnificent tomb is the only example of its type in perfect preservation. Resembling a gigantic mushroom, it has a closed chamber formed by four great slabs 5ft (1.5m) high which lean inwards and support a huge, convex capstone 12ft (3.7m) square and up to 2½ft (0.8m) thick. The chamber was investigated by W.C. Borlase in 1871, but he found nothing.

The remains of the Quoit's former covering barrow, 35ft (10.6m) in diameter, are still clearly visible. Still as much as 3ft (0.9m) high, it was of stone and part of its kerb remains on the northeast side. Large stones on the south side of the Quoit may indicate the former presence of an entrance passage.

6 Lanyon Quoit, Penwith Chamber Tomb, Madron. NT.

NG 430337. *Marked as:* **Lanyon Quoit.**
On NE side of Penzance – Morvah road 2½ miles NW of Madron.

Perhaps the best known and most photographed of all Cornwall's prehistoric monuments. Unhappily, it does not retain its original form for it was rebuilt in 1824, having been felled by a terrible storm nine years earlier. Before that, the great capstone, 17½ft (5.3m) long and 9ft (2.7m) wide, stood about 8ft (2.4m) from the ground on four upright support stones (one of which was not quite tall enough to reach the capstone). In the fall, some stones were fractured and to rebuild it in its original form was found to be impossible.

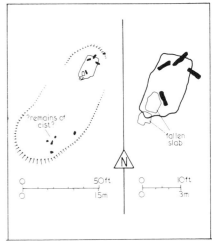

Above & below right: *Lanyon Quoit (6)*

Since the rebuilding by Captain Giddy, with the tackle that had been used to replace the famous 70-ton Logan Rock near Porthcurno *(see Site 73)*, the capstone has stood on three supports which have been shortened and squared off to a height of just over 5ft (1.5m).

The Quoit stood at the northern end of a burial mound 90ft (27m) long and 40ft (12m) broad, the outline of which is still visible. At its southern end is a collection of stones which probably formed a much smaller chamber or cist.

Dr Borlase dug beneath Lanyon Quoit in the eighteenth century and reported that, between the support stones, he had found a grave containing 'black earth'.

7 Mulfra Quoit, Penwith Chamber Tomb, New Mill.

NG 452354. *Marked as:* **Mulfra Quoit.**
Reached by footpath to the summit of Mulfra Hill, leading off W side of Penzance – Treen (North) road 1½ miles N of New Mill.

One of the smallest Penwith chamber tombs, it is now ruined and incomplete, but its original appearance must have been very similar to Chûn Quoit *(Site 5)*.

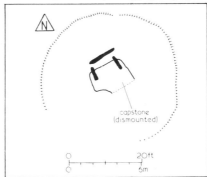

Mulfra Quoit (7)

Today, only three of the four support stones remain and, as a result, the 9½ft (2.9m) square capstone has slipped and leans sharply against the remains of the chamber which measures 6½ft (2.0m) by 5½ft (1.7m) and 5½ft high. It is not known when the fall of the capstone occurred or what happened to the fourth supporter.

The Quoit stood in the centre of a circular barrow 37ft (11m) across, but little trace of this can be seen now. Dr Borlase dug within the chamber and, as with his search at Lanyon Quoit *(Site 6)*, found a small pit containing what he described as black earth.

8 The Pennance Barrow, Scillonian Chamber Tomb, Zennor.

NG 448375. *Marked as:* **tumulus.**
In a field belonging to Pennance Farm and visible from SW side of B3306 1 mile W of Zennor.

Known locally as the 'Giant's Craw' (Cornish: *crow* – hut), this is a very well preserved entrance grave. The cone-shaped mound is 26ft (7.9m) in diameter and 6ft (1.8m) high, retained by a fine kerb of large granite blocks.

The chamber, entered from the south-east, is 13ft (4.0m) long, 4½ft (1.4m) wide and 2½ft (0.8m) high with five roofing slabs firmly in place.

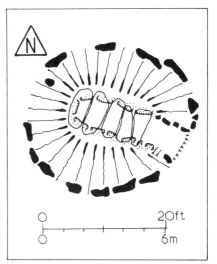

Pennance Barrow (8)

Left: *Mulfra Quoit (7). The fallen capstone can be seen clearly.*

9 Sperris Quoit, Penwith Chamber Tomb, Zennor.

NG 471382. *Not marked.*
400 yards (366m) NE of Zennor Quoit (see Site 15 for directions).

Dr Borlase wrote of a quoit close to the massive Zennor Quoit, but only in recent years was it rediscovered. Lying in the low remains of an oval barrow measuring 40ft (12m) by 26ft (8m), only a few stones remain. One, 6ft (1.8m) tall, is still standing, but the others are fallen or broken. The capstone itself is missing and was probably used in the building of two nearby mines, Wheals Sperris and Sandwich (not much remains of these, either).

Excavations by Charles Thomas in 1954 revealed a small pit which had been dug close to the remaining upright, but outside the former chamber. This held traces of a cremation burial, and other finds included flints, sherds of pottery and charcoal.

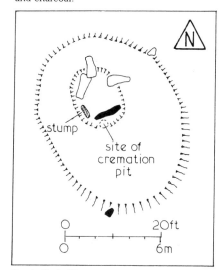

Sperris Quoit (9)

Right: *The Treen tombs (10). The well-preserved south tomb (above) and the north tomb (below).*

10 The Treen Tombs, Scillonian Chamber Tombs, Treen (North).

NG 438372. *Marked as:* **tumuli**.
In croftland on W side of Penzance – Treen road just S of its junction with B3306.

There are four barrows here, two so mutilated that it is impossible to tell whether they were ever chambered. The other two are unmistakably entrance graves.

The southern tomb is the best preserved, with a fine mound 25ft (7.6m) across and 4½ft (1.3m) high, containing a chamber 13ft (4.0m) long and 3ft (0.9m) high. The three large roof slabs are exposed at the top of the mound which has lost its retaining kerb. The chamber entrance, on the north side of the barrow, is restricted in width by two low jambstones.

The north tomb, 200ft (61m) to the north-east, is 20ft (6.1m) in diameter and just 3½ft (1.1m)

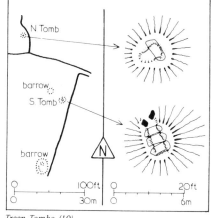

Treen Tombs (10)

high. Only the inner end of the chamber, with one roof stone remaining, is left. It was entered from the south-west.

11 The Tregeseal Barrow, Scillonian Chamber Tomb, St. Just.

NG 380322. *Not marked.*
Lane through Tregeseal leaves E side of B3306 at foot of valley just N of St. Just. Ask directions to barrow at Lower Hailglower Farm.

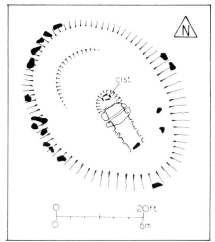

Tregeseal Barrow (11)

This rather unusual entrance grave has an oval mound 41ft (12.5m) by 31ft (9.4m) and as much as 4½ft (1.4m) high with about a third of its kerb remaining. Its chamber takes the form of a passage 11ft (3.3m) long and 4ft (1.2m) wide with an entrance, blocked by a single upright slab, facing south-east. Only the inner two roofing stones remain. It had a well-paved floor on which cremated bones, broken pottery and a small perforated whetstone were found. The excavator, in 1879, was W.C. Borlase, who also found that the mound had an inner retaining wall.

The most remarkable find was that of a small cist which had been inserted at a later date, behind the inner end of the chamber. It contained an extremely large middle Bronze Age urn which stood upside down over cremated bones. This intact urn can now be seen in the British Museum.

12 The Tregiffian Barrow, Scillonian Chamber Tomb, St. Buryan. DE.

NG 430244. *Not marked.*
On grass verge beside B3315 just W of Merry Maidens Bronze Age stone circle (see Site 30 for directions).

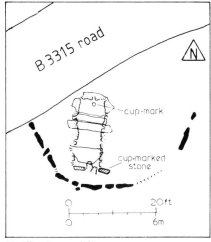

Tregiffian Barrow (12)

The large chamber of the Tregiffian Barrow (12)

Before the road cut through its northern part, this important tomb would have been about 40ft (12m) in diameter. It was first excavated by W.C. Borlase in 1871, then by the Ministry of Works (now the Department of the Environment) in 1967-8 when the barrow was threatened by a proposed road-widening scheme. Fortunately, the barrow was reprieved.

The large chamber is 14ft (4.3m) long, 4ft (1.2m) wide and 3ft (0.9m) high, retaining three very large roof stones. One of these, 11ft (3.3m) in length, was thought by Borlase to have been a fallen menhir.

The entrance to the chamber, which faced south, was blocked by a line of stones which Borlase had disturbed. Just behind these was a remarkable stone covered with artificial 'cup-marks'. A replica of this can be seen on the site; the original is in the County Museum, Truro.

The floor of the chamber, when excavated, was strewn with fragments of bone, and below the floor a pair of pits had been dug; one containing charcoal and cremated bone, the other holding an undamaged urn 15in (38cm) high.

Part of the barrow's retaining kerb still remains despite the damage which it has suffered over the years.

13 Tregiffian Vean, Scillonian Chamber Tomb, St. Just.

NG 373277. *Marked as:* **tumulus**.
Beside a track leaving W side of B3306 just N of its junction with A30. The barrow is halfway between the farms of Tregiffian and Higher Tregiffian.

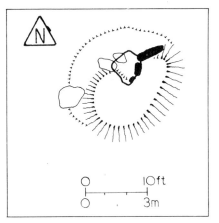

This barrow has suffered dreadfully and is only a shadow of the fine and unusual monument excavated by W.C. Borlase in 1878. It was then a kerbed mound 21ft (6.4m) in diameter, containing a rather odd-shaped chamber. This was 8ft (2.4m) long, 3ft (0.9m) wide and just 1½ft (0.5m) high, but its inner end opened out to a width of 4ft (1.2m) and a height of just over three feet (1.0m). Like the tomb at Tregeseal (*Site 11*), the entrance was blocked by a single slab. The roof of the chamber consisted of three slabs and the tomb contained ashes and an urn.

Today, this barrow is in a sorry state. All that remains of the chamber is a short passage covered by a granite slab 4½ft (1.4m) long and 4ft (1.2m) wide, supported by two stones on each side (those on the west side have fallen, one projecting from beneath the capstone). A slab on edge just to the north-east of the capstone may be in its original position. The chamber is open at the north end, the southern end being blocked by the ploughed remains of the mound which is now about 15ft (4.6m) across and just 2ft (0.6m) high.

14 West Lanyon Quoit, Penwith Chamber Tomb, Madron.

NG 423338. *Marked as:* **West Lanyon Quoit**.
Approached by footpath from lane to Little Bosullow which leaves W side of Penzance – Morvah road just N of Lanyon Farm. Path leading S from this lane crosses a stream and bears right. through fields for about 300yds (274m). The Quoit lies in the middle of a steeply sloping field.

In the nineteenth century, a farmer removed a large mound of earth and stones which lay on his land to reveal West Lanyon Quoit for the first time in 4,500 years. Unfortunately, during that time it had collapsed, and today, the fallen capstone, 13ft (4.2m) long and 10½ft (3.2m) wide, lies against the only surviving support stone, this standing 5½ft (1.6m) high. There is now no trace of the mound.

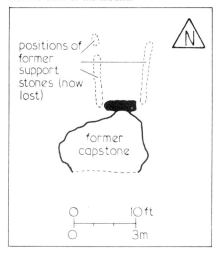

Soon after its discovery it was excavated and a number of human bones. disturbed as if the tomb had previously been rifled, were found in the ruins of the chamber.

According to tradition, the farmer who had removed the mound suffered the fate reserved for desecrators of ancient works: his cattle died and his crops failed repeatedly.

15 Zennor Quoit, Penwith Chamber Tomb, Zennor.

NG 469380. *Marked as:* **Zennor Quoit.**
Footpath leads uphill from S side of B3306 ¾ mile E of Zennor, opposite the prominent house called 'Eagle's Nest'. Keep to the path which leads straight up the slope.

This mighty tomb stands on the top of the ridge known as Zennor Carn, near the junction of two ancient trackways and, despite some irreverant treatment in the past, is an awesome sight.

Seven huge upright stones, two forming the facade to an impressive false portal and ante-chamber, support an immense capstone 18ft (5.5m) long and 9½ft (2.9m) wide, partially dismounted due to the inward collapse and breakage of the western support. This slippage

has, rather unfairly, been blamed on a Victorian farmer who, in 1861, was financially persuaded by the local vicar – a member of the Borlase family – not to break up the Quoit to build a shed, some of the stone posts of which are still standing close by. The capstone had, in fact, fallen before his time.

The chamber is 8ft (2.4m) high and the tomb once stood within a stone barrow 42ft (12.8m) in diameter, of which hardly anything remains.

In 1881, the removal of some paving slabs on the floor of the chamber, by the drastic method of blasting, revealed neolithic pottery, flints, bones and a superb perforated whetstone, the presence of which showed that the tomb had been in use well into the early Bronze Age.

Legend claims that any stone removed from the Quoit will find its own way back overnight.

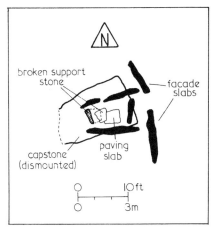

Above & below: *Zennor Quoit (15)*

The Beaker Period and the Bronze Age: 2400 – 800 BC

The intriguing Beaker people may arguably be said to belong to either the neolithic or the Bronze Age cultures. They were certainly Britain's earliest metal-users, but the copper they used they at first brought with them to Britain, or they acquired it from other peoples, rather than producing it themselves. However, it was not long after their arrival in these islands (c. 2400 BC) that they began to mine and work the metal themselves. Because they were users, and later workers of metal, this book includes them in the Bronze Age. The stone-using neolithic cultures continued for several hundred years, but gradually people absorbed the new knowledge and skills, and by 2100 BC the neolithic era was dead and the Bronze Age was staggering into life. Of course, each 'age' did not suddenly begin and end; a new era gradually took over from its predecessor.

The Beaker people, thought to have originated in the region of present-day Hungary, were another race of short people, but they were stockier and more powerful than the neolithic farmers. Judging by their broader skulls, they were perhaps less attractive in appearance than their predecessors. If the small people of Cornish legend are a folk memory of the first neolithic settlers, it may be that the ugly spriggans (a kind of goblin) were the Beaker people, and the famous Cornish giants the tall mesolithic people, or the megalith builders, who are also believed to have been a tall race.

The name 'Beaker people' stems from one of their burial practices. Many excavated Beaker skeletons were found to have been accompanied by a small pot or beaker, of which there were two main types. The bell beaker is also referred to as the AOC (all over cord) beaker, due to the fact that the pot was decorated all over by pressing two-strand twisted cord into the clay. Later, the long necked beaker, decorated with a notched comb, appeared. Geometric designs are common on these pots. The Beaker people introduced single burials under a mound (barrow) with the bodies placed in a crouched position.

When they arrived in Britain, they kept themselves apart from the neolithic folk, but as time went on they began to mix. Soon, in partnership with the megalith builders, they discovered copper deposits in Ireland and West Penwith and, from this metal, they began to manufacture flat-bladed axes. These they traded and, before long, the beginnings of a warrior aristocracy began to emerge, although as yet there is no evidence of actual warfare.

The Beaker folk clothed themselves in garments of woven wool and skin, fastened with buttons and pins of bone and copper. The women may have used copper pins to hold their hair in place. They used copper knives as well as axes, some of which were still made of stone, and featured, for the first time, a shaft-hole. These people were probably brewers as well, making a kind of barley wine. In some parts of the country, Beaker skulls have been found bearing the surprising marks of brain surgery by trepanation, probably attempts to cure such things as epilepsy, madness and migraines. Even more surprising is the fact that some people survived a number of such operations.

It is disappointing to the archaeologist that very few Beaker settlements have yet been found, and none of them in Cornwall. Nevertheless, they left other remarkable structures. It was they who built most of the *stone circles*, many of which have shown an extraordinarily competent knowledge of mathematics. The true purpose of these monuments is not known, but it seems reasonable to assume that they were for ritual and ceremonial use.

These rings of standing stones are fascinating, and few people can deny that their mysterious appearance captures the imagination in some way. Of more than twenty such circles in Cornwall, the Land's End peninsula has six, one of which raises doubts and another of which has virtually disappeared. Professor Alexander Thom has demonstrated how these circles were geometrically constructed, and possibly even astronomically designed. Some are not truly circular but of a strangely flattened shape. Of West Penwith's five appreciably remaining circles, two (Boskednan and the Merry Maidens) are true circles, the other three (Boscawen-ûn, Treen Common and Tregeseal) are of Thom's 'flattened B' design.

Many carry the name 'Nine Maidens', or similar, which is

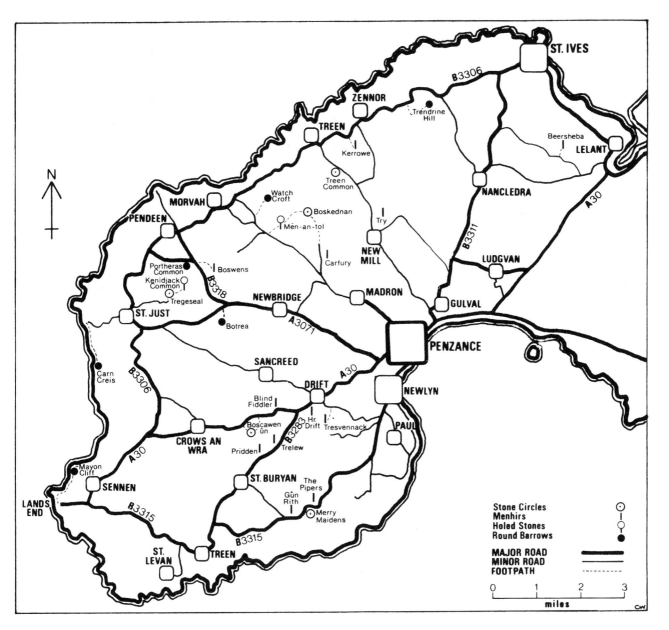

ST. IVES

B3306

ZENNOR

Trendrine
Hill

TREEN

Beersheba

LELANT

Kerrowe

NANCLEDRA

Treen
Common

A30

MORVAH

Watch
Croft

Boskednan

Try

PENDEEN

Mên-an-tol

NEW
MILL

B3311

N

Carfury

LUDGVAN

Portheras
Common

Boswens

Kenidjack
Common

B3318

NEWBRIDGE

MADRON

Tregeseal

A3071

GULVAL

ST. JUST

Botrea

PENZANCE

Carn
Creis

SANCREED

A30

B3306

DRIFT

NEWLYN

Blind
Fiddler

Hr.
Drift

Boscawen
ûn

B3283

Tresvennack

PAUL

CROWS AN
WRA

Pridden

Trelew

Mayon
Cliff

ST. BURYAN

The
Pipers

A30

Gûn
Rith

SENNEN

Merry
Maidens

LANDS
END

B3315

B3315

ST.
LEVAN

TREEN

Stone Circles
Menhirs
Holed Stones
Round Barrows

MAJOR ROAD
MINOR ROAD
FOOTPATH

0   1   2   3

miles

CW

usually explained by late Christian myths of metamorphosed sabbath-breakers, but the origin of the name may be much older. 'Maidens' may be a corruption of *mêdn*, a late spoken form of the Cornish word for stone, *mên*. The word 'nine' is something of a mystery, unless it is an abbreviation of nineteen; most of the Land's End circles appearing to have consisted of that number of stones.

With the stone circles came *menhirs*, also known as longstones (the literal translation of the Celtic word *menhyr*), monoliths or standing stones. These great upright stones are awesome objects and, again, their purpose has to be guessed at. Some may have been representations of guardian gods, others certainly marked burials. The Land's End menhirs, 37 of which are still standing, range in height from 6ft (1.8m) to the colossal 15ft (4.6m) of the north-eastern Piper of Boleigh, the tallest of the Cornish menhirs since the destruction last century of the 24ft (7.3m) Mên Pern near Constantine.

Paired menhirs are also found in West Penwith, the Pipers of Boleigh being a fine example.

Another curious type of monument found in the Land's End district is the *holed stone*. The most famous and unusual of these is the Mên-an-tol near Morvah whose beautifully cut hole is far larger than normal. There is no proof of their age but, as many are close to stone circles, menhirs and barrows, a tentative early Bronze Age date is given to them. Despite a number of theories, their purpose remains uncertain.

During the Beaker period, other groups of people were still sailing across the Channel to settle in Britain. They were mainly pastoral peoples, tending sheep and cattle and growing barley in the dryish climate with its long, warm summers. But like the neolithic people, they tended to exhaust the soil and move on to farm another spot. Little trace of settlement has been found, but, in continuation of the Beaker habit, burials were placed beneath *round barrows*, the most numerous and widespread of British prehistoric monuments.

Cremations slowly took the place of inhumation burials and the remains were often placed in a *cist*, a small box of stone slabs. At this time, there was still generally only one burial in each barrow. Funeral rites were long and complex. To start with, the body would lie in state, often until the flesh decayed, when it was burnt on a funeral pyre. The bones were washed and put in a cist, an urn or a leather bag. After feasting which often lasted days, the barrow was built over the remains. In stony areas like West Penwith, these barrows would normally be kerbed by large stone blocks.

Early Bronze Age clothing was mostly of wool. Men wore long skirts starting from below the shoulders and tied at the waist. Over this would be a poncho-like cape, and the common headgear was a round, close-fitting woollen cap. Women wore long dresses with half-length sleeves in winter. In summer they would wear a thin, square-necked jumper and a corded skirt fastened by a belt, often with a circular plate-metal fastener. Their hair was kept in place with long pins of jet, copper or bone, and they too often wore a cap or a net. Jewellery was in fashion; women's graves frequently contained earrings of gold and bronze. Male burials were often accompanied by knives, arrowheads and battleaxes.

Circa 1900 BC, small groups of warriors and tin merchants from what is now Brittany started to set up home in Britain, and to begin a prosperous trade in bronze, an alloy of tin and copper. The discovery of bronze-making techniques in Britain probably happened in the Land's End peninsula, near St. Just, where the ores of both tin and copper occur naturally together. The enterprising new settlers took full advantage of their discovery and soon became powerful enough to dominate the population. Recognising the flair of the Beaker people, they persuaded them to join forces in working and exporting Cornish tin and copper, as well as Irish gold and copper, to Brittany and the Mediterranean, acting both as producers and middle-men. The venture was a complete success and the new arrivals became a rich, powerful society throughout southern Britain. They are known to archaeologists as the *Wessex Culture*.

In the middle of the second millenium BC, Mycenaean Greece was demanding more of these metals than her Mediterranean neighbours could produce, and Britain proved to be the answer to her problem. Word spread and soon, not only was Mycenae buying from the Wessex Culture, but Crete, Brittany, the Baltic countries and northern Germany. The wealth of the Wessex Culture produced a class society: at the top were the aristocratic chieftains and their ladies, then a warrior class and, below them, the poorer working classes.

Wessex Culture burials were also under round barrows, but these people began to design different architectural types: the simple *bowl barrow*, just a mound like an upturned bowl, usually with a ditch around it, was the most common. The *bell barrow* had its surrounding ditch separated from the mound by a flat platform, or berm. Two other types found in West Penwith are the *disc barrow* and the *ring barrow*. The first of these has an extremely small mound surrounded by a wide, flat space, then an encircling bank and ditch. The ring barrow is simply a circular bank and ditch. It is common to find more than one burial in Wessex Culture barrows.

The pottery produced by these people can be divided into two classes; *food vessels*: wide, bowl-shaped and often heavily decorated pots; and *collared urns*: tall vessels with a decorated collar around the wide neck. Both types have been found in Cornwall.

By 1400 BC, the Wessex Culture had collapsed. Two factors combined to bring about their downfall. First, the British climate deteriorated fairly sharply, becoming cooler and wetter, which caused a certain amount of confusion. Although barrow-burial continued, the old religion and its trappings, the stone circles, menhirs and henges, were abandoned. Even the advanced astronomical and mathematical knowledge was forgotten. It seems as if the old gods and beliefs were completely abandoned to make way for new ones. Secondly, and most importantly, the Wessex traders lost their two major customers: Mycenae and Crete. The reason for this was the colossal eruption of the volcanic island of Thera, or Santorini, in the Aegean Sea, the tidal waves and convulsions from which decimated their trading fleets, ending the maritime domination of the renowned 'sea kings' of Crete.

Another type of pottery now became widespread in Britain.

Known as *deveral-rimbury* ware, it was coarse and inferior compared with the food vessels and collared urns of the Wessex Culture. It was as if the whole of British society in the Bronze Age had taken a backward step. This pottery came in barrel, bucket and globular shapes decorated with the fingertips or with bands of clay. It was used mainly as domestic ware, but also turns up in burials.

Although the building of round barrows still went on, it was becoming more common to inter the dead in flat cemeteries or to use existing barrows. Grave goods became rare.

By 1200 BC, farming techniques had improved sufficiently to see the beginning of permanent settlement. The dwelling type of the period, known as the *hut circle*, continued throughout the coming Iron Age and will be described under that section. Apart from their cereal crops, the farmers of the middle and late Bronze Age tended sheep, cattle, goats and pigs, and by then the horse was in use, both for drawing wheeled carts and for riding and rounding up cattle.

Four hundred years later, the Bronze Age was drawing to a close. Gradually, new people were appearing in Britain, bringing with them new ideas, new methods and knowledge of a new metal: iron.

Bronze Age monuments which can be seen in the Land's End peninsula are of four main types: stone circles, menhirs, holed stones and round barrows. The following list includes the best of these sites.

16 The Beersheba Menhir, Lelant.

NG 525371. *Marked as:* **standing stone.**
Near footpath leading N from the Bowl Rock at Trevarrack.

Known locally as the 'Longstone', this stone is a fine example of its type. Solid and regular in shape, it stands 10ft (3.0m) tall. No excavations have taken place here.

17 The Blind Fiddler, Menhir, Drift.

NG 425282. Marked as: **The Blind Fiddler – standing stone.**
Behind hedge skirting N side of A30, about 1 mile W of Drift.

Also known as the Trenuggo or Tregonebris Stone, this magnificent menhir is a great upright slab of quartz-studded granite 11ft (3.3m) high. Early nineteenth-century excavations near its foot uncovered fragments of bone.

   The stone gets its popular name from eighteenth-century Methodist parables, local preachers instructing their wayward flock that here stands a stricken musician, turned to stone for performing on a Sunday.

Above: *The Blind Fiddler menhir (17)*

18 Boscawen-ûn Stone Circle, St. Buryan.

NG 412274. Marked as: **stone circle.**
Reached along farm track through Boscawen-noon farm, leading S off A30 1 mile W of Drift.

Boscawen-ûn, or the 'Nine Maidens', is one of Cornwall's finest stone circles. Nineteen upright stones, from 3 to 4½ft (0.9-1.4m) high, form an ingeniously constructed ellipse with diameters of 80ft (24.4m) and 71ft (21.7m), now standing within a modern enclosure. Within the ring, but set somewhat off-centre, is a stone 8ft (2.4m) tall which leans sharply towards the north-east where a pair of flat slabs lies on the edge of the circle. These were thought by Dr Borlase to have been part of a burial cist. All the circle's stones are of granite, except for one on the western quadrant and to the south of an entrance gap. This stone is a block of almost pure quartz.

   The stone circle appears to have been used as recently as the Dark Ages, for the ancient Welsh triads name a 'Beisgawen yn Dumnonia' as the site of one of the three principal gorsedds (bardic meeting-places) of the Island of Britain. (In 1928, the Gorsedd of the Bards of Cornwall was inaugurated at this stone circle, and has continued annually since then, but held at a different site each year. A special Gorsedd, to mark its fiftieth anniversary, was held at Boscawen-ûn in September 1978.)

   To the north-east of the stone circle are two outlying menhirs. The nearest, 400yds (366m) away at NG 415276 (*marked as:* **standing stone**), is an upright pillar 8½ft (2.6m) high, close to which is a long, prostrate stone built into the hedge. This may once have stood nearby to form one of a pair similar to that at Higher Drift *(see Site 25)*.

   The other menhir which still stands is a bulky, conical stone 7½ft (2.3m) high which juts out of the hedge bordering the lane leading from the A30 to Boscawen-noon farm at NG 417277 *(not marked)*.

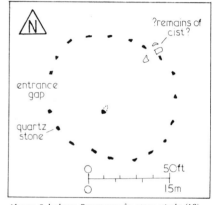

Above & below: *Boscawen-ûn stone circle (18)*

19 Boskednan Stone Circle, Madron.

NG 434351. *Marked as:* **Nine Maidens – stone circle.**
Reached by continuing along the track past the Mên-an-tol (see Site 29 for directions) and bearing right at the end of the track up to the brow of the moorland ridge. Alternatively, a lane to Ding Dong Mine (signposted) leaves the Penzance – Morvah road 1 ½ miles NW of Madron. From the mine's disused engine house, a footpath leads N to the circle. BEWARE OF MINE SHAFTS.

Another 'Nine Maidens', this ruined circle could hardly be in a lonelier spot. 69ft (21m) across, it retains eleven stones from a probable original of nineteen. Seven of these still stand although one or two lean alarmingly. The upright stone on the north side of the circle is unusually large compared with stones in other local circles, being 7ft (2.1m) high.

The remains of a round barrow, clearly later than the circle, intrude into its southern side. 33ft (10m) in diameter and 4ft (1.2m) high, it contains the remains of a central cist in which an urn and sherds of pottery were found by W.C. Borlase in 1872. Two excavation trenches can still be seen, a technique which would be deplored today.

Three more barrows lie to the north of the circle, one of which, standing prominently on the summit of the ridge, has a ring of leaning stones on it. These are the remains of its retaining kerb which now protrudes from the almost disintegrated mound.

Beside the path and 60yds (55m) north of the circle is the site of a former outlying menhir. All that remains is a stump 1ft (0.3m) high.

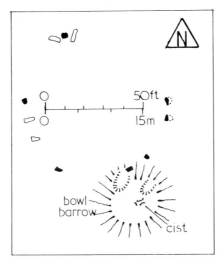

20 The Boswens Menhir, Pendeen.

NG 400329. *Marked as:* **standing stone.**
On open moorland and visible from E side of B3318 1 mile S of Pendeen.

This 8½ft (2.6m) high menhir stands high on the north-eastern slope of Dry Carn and in the centre of an extremely low barrow 40ft (12.2m) in diameter. Chûn Castle Iron Age hill fort *(Site 54)* and Chûn Quoit Neolithic Penwith Chamber Tomb *(Site 5)* are both visible from this site.

21 Botrea Round Barrows, Newbridge.

NG 403312. *Marked as:* **tumuli.**
On hilltop immediately S of junction of A3071 and B3318.

Four large disc-barrows, from 53ft (16m) to 118ft (36m) across, and up to 5ft (1.5m) high, lie in a north-south line on the flat summit of Botrea Hill. Three of them have been explored, finds including ashes, a cist containing an urn and another cist in which were two fine barbed arrowheads.

Three bowl-barrows, two of which are very large, lie just to the south-east of the southern-most disc-barrow. One of these also yielded an urn.

22 Carfury Menhir, Madron.

NG 440340. *Not marked.*
Just off, and downhill from, the top of the lane leading from the Penzance – Morvah road to Ding Dong Mine.

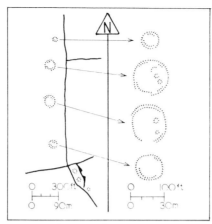

Botrea Round Barrows (21)

This little-known but superb menhir stands on a steep hillside with its base embedded in a low and extremely old wall. Elegant and perhaps partly shaped, its height is 10ft (3.0m).

The ground at its foot was excavated in 1958 by Vivien Russell and Peter Pool, but nothing was found.

23 Carn Creis Round Barrows, St. Just.

NG 357297. *Not marked.*
Beside cliff path between Penanwell (Porth Nanven on map) and Whitesand Bay, just S of Polpry Cove.

Two barrows stand on the clifftop and both were excavated by W.C. Borlase in 1878. The northern barrow, on the landward side of the path, is 33ft (10m) in diameter and parts of both inner and outer retaining walls can still be seen. A cist was found in the centre of the barrow and a flat slab lying on the eastern edge of the mound may have been its capstone. Sherds of pottery were also uncovered.

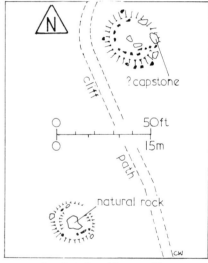

Carn Creis Round Barrows (23)

The southern mound, only 23ft (7m) across, yielded an astonishing range of finds. This had been a kerbed ring mound raised around a natural boulder 4ft (1.2m) high, and within it were four urns, three of them dating from the middle Bronze Age, along with other fragments of pottery, a perforated stone, a leaf-shaped arrowhead, shale discs, pieces of glass, a steatite button and a number of segmented faience beads.

24 Gûn Rith Menhir, St. Buryan.

NG 429245. *Not marked.*
In hedge of field across road from Tregiffian neolithic Scillonian chamber tomb (see Sites 12 and 30 for directions).

Also known as the 'Fiddler', this outlier of the Merry Maidens stone circle *(Site 30)* is 10½ft (3.2m) tall and leans slightly outward from the hedge.

W.C. Borlase excavated the foot of the stone in 1871, but his only find was a beach pebble.

25 Higher Drift Menhirs, Drift.

NG 437283. *Marked as:* **standing stones.**
In a field adjoining S side of A30 just W of Drift.

This fine pair of standing stones, 7½ft (2.3m) and 9ft (2.7m) high and 18ft (5.5m) apart, is visible from the road. They were investigated by W.C. Borlase in 1871 and it was found that a grave had been dug between them, although not in direct line. No other finds were made. These menhirs have various names, including the 'Sisters' and the Triganeeris Stones.

26 Kenidjack Common Holed Stones, St. Just.

NG 390326. *Not marked.*
Beside a path leading NE from Tregeseal stone circle (see Site 35 for directions) and on open moorland 300yds (274m) SE of Carn Kenidjack.

There are five holed stones here; three forming a close alignment orientated WSW-ENE and two outliers. The north-east outlier, 100yds (91m) from the alignment, is 3ft (0.9m) high with a hole of 7in (18cm) diameter carved through it.

The eastern stone of the alignment is 4½ft (1.4m) high with a 3½in (9cm) hole. Between this and the next stone is another, apparently part of the row, but unperforated. The next holed stone has fallen but would have been 4ft

Top: *Gûn Rith menhir (24).* Centre: *Higher Drift menhirs (25).* Below right: *Kenidjack Common holed stones (26).*

(1.2m) high. It has a 3in (7.6cm) diameter hole, and the western stone, 2½ft (0.8m) high, also has a 3in hole.

The north-western outlier, about 20yds (18m) from this last stone, is also 2½ft high and with a 3in hole. Both outlying stones have fractured horizontally across the hole but their tops are now back in place.

Like the Mên-an-tol *(Site 29)* and the Boleigh holed stone, close to the Merry Maidens *(Site 30)*, these holed stones are within sight of a stone circle, round barrows and menhirs.

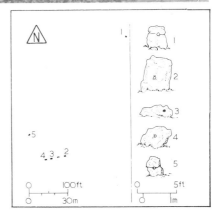

27 Kerrowe Menhir, Zennor.

NG 452373. *Not marked.*
At end of track S from Kerrowe Farm on B3306 ½ mile SW of Zennor.

This small, stout menhir, 6½ft (1.9m) high, was excavated by the West Cornwall Field Club in 1935. Near its foot, two late Bronze Age urns were uncovered, one placed inside the other and standing on a heap of charcoal. Close by were traces of a late Bronze and early Iron Age settlement, of which two hut circles, along with their associated system of terraced fields, can still be seen.

28 Mayon Cliff Round Barrows, Sennen. NT.

NG 349260. *Not marked.*
By cliff path just S of coastguard lookout on Pedn-mên-du.

The most prominent of these two barrows stands immediately beside the cliff path as it leads south towards Land's End. 26ft (7.9m) in diameter and 2ft (0.6m) high, it still has much of its kerb although most of the mound has gone. The roofless remains of a large cist are exposed to view.

The second barrow is a low mound 30ft (9.1m) in diameter and is 50yd (46m) north-east of its

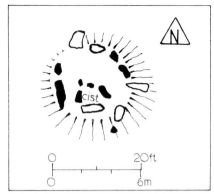

Mayon Cliff Round Barrows (28)

neighbour. These are probably the two barrows on Mayon Cliff excavated by W.C. Borlase in 1879, but nothing was found in either.

29 Mên-an-Tol, Holed Stone, Morvah.

NG 426349. *Marked as:* **Men-an-tol.**
Reached by signposted track off NE side of Penzance – Morvah road at Bosullow Common, opposite turning to Chûn Castle Iron Age hill fort (Site 54).

This mysterious monument consists of four stones; one fallen stone, two uprights 4½ft (1.3m) high and, between these and in direct line with them, a wheel-shaped slab set firmly on its rim. This is 4ft (1.2m) across and is pierced by a large round hole 20in (51cm) in diameter, large enough for a grown man to crawl through (and most do!). This slab is the Mên-an-tol itself. The name is pure Cornish and means simply, stone of the hole.

Although the three erect stones are now in line, this is not the original layout; it is known that at least one of the stones has been moved in recent times and that they once formed a triangle.

The purpose of the Mên-an-tol is quite unknown, although theories abound. The most common of these is that the stone was the porthole entrance to a vanished megalithic tomb. But this seems most unlikely since no

other Cornish tomb has such a thing. The Mên-an-tol is a total mystery and is likely to remain one for a very long time.

Like other holed stones in the district, it is within sight of a stone circle – the Boskednan Nine Maidens can be seen on the skyline to the east – round barrows and two menhirs, the Boswens Stone *(Site 20)* and one on the summit of Watch Croft *(see Site 40).*

The Mên-an-tol is sometimes called the Crick Stone, for the ritual of crawling through the hole nine times widdershins was said to cure rickets and scrofula. It was also believed that if two brass pins were placed crosswise on the stone, questions would be answered by a mysterious movement of the pins.

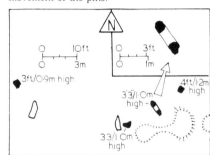

Mên-an-Tol holed stone (29)

30 The Merry Maidens, Stone Circle, St. Buryan.

NG 433245. *Marked as:* **Merry Maidens – stone circle.**
In a field adjoining S side of B3315 ¾ mile SW of the Lamorna valley.

Probably the best known stone circle in Cornwall, this fine monument is also one of the most perfect. 78ft (24m) in diameter, it is a true and complete circle of nineteen upright stones between 3 and 4½ft (0.9m and 1.4m) tall. A gap on the eastern side was probably the entrance. The site is also known as the Boleigh or Rosemodress circle and as the Dawns Mên (Cornish: *dons meyn* – dance of stones).

Like most other stone circles in the area, the Merry Maidens have barrows, holed stones and menhirs in the immediate vicinity, including the massive pair of standing stones called the Pipers of Boleigh *(Site 31)* and the Gûn Rith stone *(Site 24)*, which can be seen from the circle (the Pipers cannot).

A very fine holed stone can be seen on the opposite side of the road at NG 432246. Now used as a gatepost, it is 5½ft (1.6m) high with a 6in (15cm) diameter hole near its top.

The late T.C. Lethbridge presented a fascinating report after trying to determine the circle's age by means of a dowsing pendulum.

He wrote that he felt a tingling sensation, like a mild electric shock, from the stone he was touching. He also reported that, at the same time, he felt the stone rocking and swaying wildly, even though it was firmly bedded in the ground. The result of his dating by dowsing was *c.* 2540 BC, uncannily close to its latest generally accepted date of 2400 BC.

31 The Pipers of Boleigh, Menhirs, St. Buryan.

NG 435248. *Marked as:* **The Pipers – standing stones.**
On NW side of B3315 ¼ mile NE of Merry Maidens stone circle (Site 30).

The north-east Piper, that nearest Boleigh Farm, is, at 15ft (4.6m), Cornwall's tallest menhir. Its companion, 317ft (99m) away and in the next field, runs second in the league at 13½ft (4.1m).

Both underwent fruitless examinations by W.C. Borlase in 1871.

A line drawn from one Piper to the other and extended south-west would touch a stone on the north-west quadrant of the Merry Maidens, adding weight to the highly probable theory that these stones are of Bronze Age origin and part of the stone circle's system of outlying monuments. There is a tradition that they were peace stones erected by King Athelstan after he had subdued Howal, the last Cornish king, in a supposed battle here in AD 931, but this is unlikely.

Below: *Pipers of Boleigh (31):* left, *north-east menhir,* and right, *south-west menhir.*

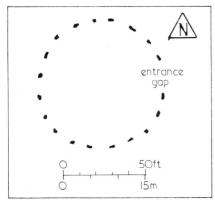

Above & top right: *Merry Maidens stone circle (30)*

32 Portheras Common Round Barrow, Pendeen.

NG 391333. *Not marked.*
In a small triangular plot of moorland beside the Trewellard branch of the B3318 near its junction with the Pendeen branch of the same road.

A very fine barrow, 40ft (12.2m) in diameter and 2½ft (0.8m) high, with much of its stone kerb remaining. In the centre of the mound is a well-preserved burial cist 4ft (1.2m) long and 2ft (0.6m) wide, roofed by a heavy capstone some 6ft (1.8m) long.

It is believed to have been excavated by W.C. Borlase, and a cupped stone (present whereabouts unknown) probably came from this barrow.

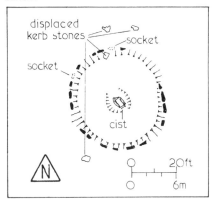

Portheras Common Round Barrow (32)

33 Pridden Menhir, St. Buryan.

NG 417266. *Not marked.*
Situated at corner of hedge just NE of Pridden Farm, 1 mile NE of St. Buryan. Visible from NW side of B3283.

This unusual stone, a great slab 9ft (2.7m) in height, stood upright in 1871 when W.C. Borlase dug at its base, but now, perhaps as a result of his dig, it leans sharply away from the hedge.

Borlase found that the stone had been set just

6in (15cm) into the ground, and he discovered human bone fragments and ashes in a pit covered by a granite slab near the southern foot of the menhir.

34 Treen Common Stone Circle, Treen (North).

NG 445367. *Marked as:* **enclosure.**
By W side of Penzance – Gurnard's Head road 2 miles N of New Mill.

Little known and little mentioned, this curious monument consists of an irregular, elliptical ring of 14 erect and numerous fallen stones, the diameters of which are 110ft (33m) and 99ft (30m). The stones are irregularly spaced, from 1ft (0.3m) to 4½ft (1.4m) high, and set on a low bank some 20ft (6.1m) wide. The entrance to the ring appears to be on the eastern side of the tallest stone, this being on the south-eastern quadrant of the circle.

The site, Dr. Borlase's 'Zennor Cirque', has not been excavated and raises doubts as to what it is. It may well be an unusual form of Bronze Age

stone circle or perhaps even a late form of the neolithic henge. Equally possible is the suggestion that it represents the ruined ring-wall of a vanished Iron Age settlement, especially since it stands in the midst of a large prehistoric field system, hardly traceable from ground level but clearly seen from the air.

To the south, on the top of the hill, are three round barrows. The north-westerly mound, 52ft (15.8m) across and 3ft (0.9m) high, and the central barrow, about the same height and 35ft (10.6m) in diameter, are clearly visible, the latter retaining much of its kerb. Both were excavated by W.C. Borlase in 1872, finds including ashes, flint and a fragment of iron. Just to the south-east of these are the low, scanty remnants of a ring barrow known as the 'Beacon', which is 50ft (15.2m) in diameter.

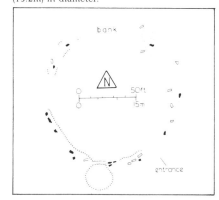

Treen Common Stone Circle (34)

35 Tregeseal Stone Circle, St. Just.

NG 387324. *Marked as:* **stone circle.**
Reached by lanes E from B3306 ½ mile N of St. Just, or by footpath from Botallack.

Variously known as the Nine Maidens or Dancing Stones, the Tregeseal circle lies on the southern fringe of a moor dominated by the rugged and sinister Carn Kenidjack.

This lonely circle is of a slightly flattened design, its diameters being 69ft (21m) and 72ft (22m). It has nineteen stones, from 2½ft (0.8m) to 5ft (1.5m) high; one is prone and many others have been re-erected in recent years.

It was once the eastern circle of a line of three, similar to the famous Hurlers near Liskeard. The western circle disappeared centuries ago and its site was found only by examining crop-marks on aerial photographs. The central circle was in the field nearby, four of its stones (one on edge) still in place but incorporated into the hedge just west of the

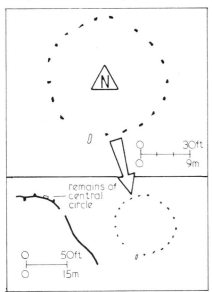

Above & top right: *Tregeseal stone circle (35)*

field gate. The remainder of the circle was wantonly destroyed by the then landowner in 1961, who maintained that it was 'in the way'.

To the north of the circle are a number of round barrows, two of which are outstanding. Both are beside the path leading north-east towards the Kenidjack Common holed stones

36 Trelew Menhir, St. Buryan.

NG 422269. *Not marked.*
In field beside track to Trelew Farm, which leads off NW side of B3283 1½ miles NE of St. Buryan.

This 10ft (3.0m) tall, top-heavy menhir was excavated by W.C. Borlase in 1871. He found that a pit had been dug some 3ft (0.9m) north of the stone which contained pieces of wood, flint, clay and some calcined bone. For some strange reason, this menhir had been erected on its narrowest end.

37 Trendrine Hill Round Barrows, Zennor.

NG 479387. *Not marked.*
On summit of Trendrine Hill, best reached by track leading uphill from B3306 1½ miles E of Zennor to Sperris Croft Iron Age hut settlement (Site 71) then bearing E along the ridge to the hilltop.

Two very large and prominent barrows stand on the hilltop, the largest of which is a great cairn of stones 62ft (19m) across and 8½ft (2.5m)

(Site 26). The nearest, 40ft (12.2m) in diameter and 5½ft (1.6m) high, has part of its kerb remaining and may have held a cist. The next barrow, 46ft (14m) across and 5ft (1.5m) high, has the remains of a stone chamber which may have been an entrance grave (Scillonian chamber tomb).

Trelew Menhir (36)

high, now topped by an Ordnance Survey triangulation pillar.

Just to the south is another large mound 46ft (14m) in diameter and 6½ft (2.0m) high, with a kerb of extremely large stones which include natural outcrops. Parts of an inner retaining wall are also visible as are the remains of a central cist.

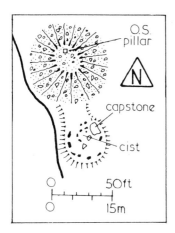

39 Try Menhir,
New Mill.

NG 460350. *Not marked.*
In field 200yds (183m) S of Try Farm, reached from E side of Penzance – Gurnard's Head road 1 mile N of New Mill.

The shapely 9ft (2.7m) tall menhir was excavated in 1958 and 1962 by Vivien Russell and Peter Pool. A stone cist with a massive capstone was found buried near the foot of the stone. Originally covered by a small cairn, the cist contained a 'Handled A' beaker, various fragments of pottery and bones, both calcined and unburnt. Around the cist were scattered sherds and flints, and a saddle quern was also uncovered. The beaker can be seen in the County Museum, Truro.

A slight mound between the two barrows is the remnant of a third, which may also have contained a cist.

Above: *Plan and photograph of Trendrine Hill Barrows (37)*

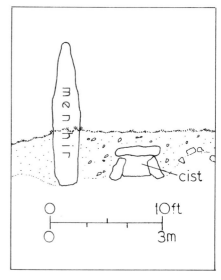

Try Menhir (39).

38 The Tresvennack Pillar, Menhir,
Drift.

NG 442279. *Not marked.*
Ask for directions at Tresvennack Farm, off side road from A30 at Drift to B3318 at Chywoone Grove.

One of the finest of the Cornish menhirs, this tall, elegant stone is 11½ft (3.5m) high and set 4ft (1.2m) into the ground.

It was investigated by the farmer in 1840, who discovered a large stone slab buried some 2ft (0.6m) south of the stone. The slab covered a pit, cut into the subsoil, which contained two middle Bronze Age urns, one of which was extremely large and held cremated human bones. The other contained a powdery substance. Both urns can be seen in the museum at Penlee House, Penzance.

Left: *One of the best examples of the Cornish menhirs, the Tresvennack Pillar (38).*

40 Watch Croft Round Barrows and Menhir, Morvah.

NG 420357. *Not marked.*
On summit of Watch Croft, best reached from the Penzance – Morvah road. BEWARE OF MINE SHAFTS to the north and west of the summit.

The most prominent barrow on the hill is a stone cairn 66ft (20m) in diameter and 8ft (2.4m) high, with an Ordnance Survey triangulation pillar on the top. It is said that some pottery was turned up when the pillar was erected.

Just to the south-west is a natural outcrop of rock with the remains of an old shelter built against its southern face. Loose stones can be seen heaped around the base of this outcrop and it is suspected to have been the site of a barrow, although W.C. Borlase, who excavated it in 1863, found nothing.

Close by is a small, leaning menhir 6½ft (1.9m) tall, also examined by Borlase in 1863 but, again, with no result.

He had better luck with a fine stone barrow 300yds (274m) to the south, among small rock outcrops at NG 419355. 50ft (15.2m) in diameter and 6ft (1.8m) high, this extraordinary structure is a cairn built over natural rocks and surrounded by a beautifully built retaining wall up to three courses high. This also made use of naturally outcropping rock. Borlase found a cist in the centre of the barrow, holding a late Bronze Age urn which contained calcined bones.

The most intriguing find to emerge from this barrow was a number of Roman coins from the reign of Constantine, now to be seen in Truro Museum. They were found deep inside the barrow, which showed no sign of having been disturbed previously, and it is interesting to imagine how these coins got there.

Above: *The stone cairn and menhir at the Watch Croft barrows site (40).*

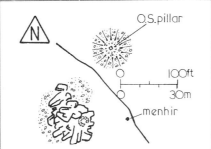

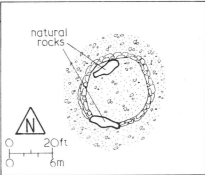

The Iron Age:
800 BC – AD 410

The Cornish Iron Age began to take over from the Bronze Age *circa* 800 BC. Apart from its last few centuries, the Bronze Age is looked upon as the 'Age of the Dead', for most of its remaining monuments are funerary or ritual structures. In complete contrast, the Iron Age is very much the 'Age of the Living', its remains are of dwelling sites and defensive positions.

The first iron-using people to arrive in Britain probably belonged to what is known as the Iron Age A or Hallstatt culture, but their influence on Cornwall was slight. It was the people of the Iron Age B, or La Tene, culture who made the greatest impression. They were the Celts; tall, powerful, clannish people who had originated in the area of the Alps, spreading east and west and appearing in Greek and Roman records as 'Keltoi', 'Galatians' and Gauls'. They were skilled farmers, mariners, craftsmen and warriors, making great use of iron, stronger and easier to fashion than bronze, in the manufacture of their edge tools and weapons. Bronze, of course, was still an important metal and was used for decorative and domestic ware. Celtic swords were iron-bladed, often with bronze hilts. Shields were also fashioned from bronze.

Cornish tin was once again the source of valuable trade, and it was in all likelihood to guard the precious mining area that the Celts ringed the Land's End peninsula with cliff castles and hill forts. This famous Cornish tin trade was of great interest to the Greek geographer Pytheas of Massilia (Marseilles, then a Greek colony), who visited Penwith – known to the Greeks as Belerion – shortly before 300 BC. Although his own annals have been lost, he was faithfully quoted by the first century BC Sicilian-Greek historian Diodorus Siculus, so here we have one of the oldest written records of Britain; a factual account of Penwith and its tin trade, and a remarkable illustration of Iron Age life:

> The people of that promontory of Britain called Belerion are friendly to strangers and, from their contact with foreign merchants, are civilised in their way of life. They carefully work the ground from which they extract the tin. It is rocky but contains earthy veins, the produce of which they grind down, smelt and purify. The metal is then beaten into ingots shaped like astragali and

> carried to a certain island lying off the coast of Britain which is called Iktis. During the ebb of the tide, the intervening space is left dry and they carry the tin, in abundance, over to this island in their wagons. Here, then, the merchants buy the tin from the natives and carry it over to Gaul and, after travelling overland for about thirty days, they finally bring their loads on horseback to the mouth of the Rhone.

The island of Iktis is almost certainly St. Michael's Mount and it is known that the 'foreign merchants' were the Veneti, Breton Celts closely related to the Cornish. The popular notion that the Phoenicians came to Cornwall for tin is nothing more than a myth which sprung up in the seventeenth century. Its novelty made it attractive, and it is still believed although there is not a scrap of archaeological evidence to support it.

What did the Iron Age inhabitants of Belerion look like? Small, dark-haired, fine-featured people descended from neolithic stock; small, heavier men descended from the Beaker folk of the early Bronze Age; taller, fairer people, not unlike the Celts themselves, whose forefathers had built the great megalithic tombs 2,000 years before: all these were still here, although greatly intermixed. The Celts themselves were tall, well-built people. It is often said that they were fair-haired, but this is not strictly so. Diodorus Siculus, describing the Celts of Gaul, wrote that, '. . . their hair is blond but not naturally so: they bleach it by washing it in lime and combing it back from their foreheads . . . thick and shaggy like a horse's mane', to present a terrifying appearance in battle. In peacetime they almost certainly left their hair its natural colour, which in many cases was blond, although dark- and red-haired Celts were just as common. Men and women wore their hair long, and the men were often bearded or heavily moustached.

Their clothes were brightly coloured, striped and checked patterns predominating in their high-quality woven textiles. It is interesting to note that tweed originated in the Iron Age. The men wore trousers, belted or with drawstrings at the waist and ankle, a round-necked tunic shirt and a woollen, calf-length cloak which fastened at the shoulder by an exquisitely fashioned brooch pin. Shoes were mostly similar to the moccasin, but sandals and well made hide boots were also worn. Women wore long dresses, belted at the waist, and cloaks in cold or adverse weather. Their hair was often plaited, the plaits worn loose or coiled about the head and held in place by a bronze pin.

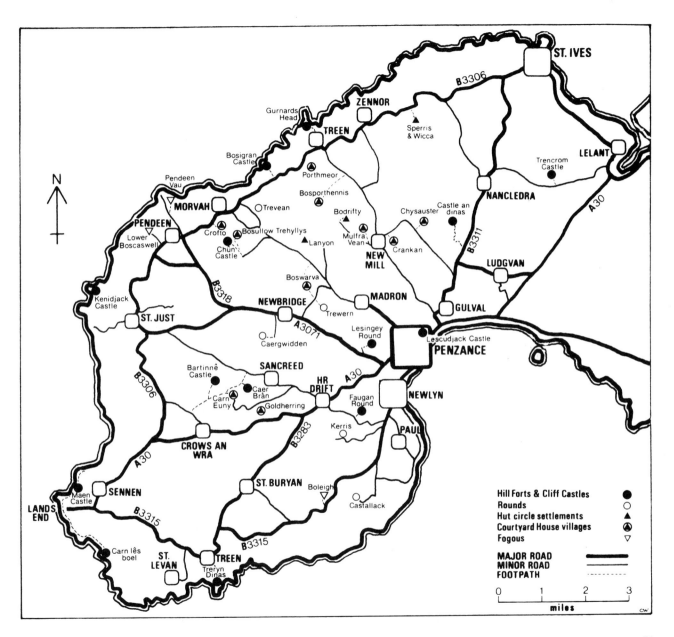

N

ST. IVES

B3306

ZENNOR

Gurnards
Head

TREEN

Sperris
& Wicca

LELANT

Bosigran
Castle

Porthmeor

Trencrom
Castle

Pendeen
Vau

Bosporthennis

NANCLEDRA

A30

MORVAH

Trevean

Bodrifty

Chysauster

Castle an
dinas

PENDEEN

Crofto

Bosullow Trehyllys

Mulfra
Vean

Lanyon

Crankan

B3311

Lower
Boscaswell

Chûn
Castle

NEW
MILL

LUDGVAN

Boswarva

Kenidjack
Castle

B3318

NEWBRIDGE

MADRON

GULVAL

ST. JUST

A3071

Trewern

Lesingey
Round

Lescudjack Castle

Caergwidden

PENZANCE

Bartinné
Castle

SANCREED

HR
DRIFT

A30

NEWLYN

B3306

Carn
Euny

Caer
Brân

Goldherring

Faugan
Round

Kerris

PAUL

CROWS AN
WRA

A30

B3283

ST. BURYAN

Boleigh

Castallack

SENNEN

Maen
Castle

B3315

LANDS
END

Carn lês
boel

ST.
LEVAN

B3315

TREEN

Treryn
Dinas

Hill Forts & Cliff Castles ●
Rounds ○
Hut circle settlements ▲
Courtyard House villages ⊕
Fogous ▽

MAJOR ROAD
MINOR ROAD
FOOTPATH

0   1   2   3
miles

CW

31

Both sexes favoured jewellery: wristlets, armlets, torcs and brooches were among their superbly made ornaments of bronze and gold, sometimes inlaid with coloured enamel and decorated with the beautiful flowing curves and circles typical of La Tene artwork. Accessories such as mirrors and combs were also in wide use. The Celts of south western Britain used no currency until well into the Roman period, preferring instead to barter for necessities.

Religion was as complex as were the many Celtic gods, among them Dagda, or Good Father; Belenos the sun-god; Taranis the thunderer; horned Cernunnos, lord of the underworld; and Teutates, protector of the people. The Earth Mother was highly revered and even animals had their divine protectors, like Epona the horse goddess, who gives us our modern word 'pony'. The Celtic priests were the Druids, who also acted as the wise men and recorders. No records were written down. The Druids held them in their memories, handing them down by word of mouth. Initiates were recruited almost exclusively from the warrior classes and faced long, gruelling periods of instruction.

The Celtic year was divided into four seasons, with festivals held on the first day of each. *Samain* (1 November) was the Celtic New Year, on the eve of which supernatural events were believed to take place. *Imbolc* (1 February) was at lambing time and *Beltane* (1 May), dedicated to Belenos, was a time for bonfires through which cattle were driven to purify them and protect them from disease. Finally there was *Lughnasa* (1 August), a harvest festival.

The major occupations of the people of Iron Age Penwith were agriculture and the extraction, processing and trading of tin. Remains of their tiny, irregularly shaped fields with their stone walls (locally 'hedges') can be seen all over the Land's End peninsula, and many are still in use today, especially along the coastal strip between Morvah and Zennor. Where slopes were steep, the Celtic farmers terraced their fields into the hillside. Some fields and hedges in West Penwith are even older than this, dating well back into the Bronze Age. Farming was mixed. Short-horned cattle had taken over from the longer-horned varieties favoured by the Bronze Age farmers. Sheep and pigs were kept, as were the native breeds of pony and horses bred from imported strains. The principal crops were wheat, barley, oats, rye, lentils, peas and flax. Hay, of course, was also cultivated as fodder for the farm animals which included the oxen used for drawing the farmer's plough.

Tin-mining was again coming into its own. Extraction was by streaming and open-cast digging. After the careful purification and smelting described by Diodorus, the tin ingots were carried by pack-horse and wagon along the ridgeways to the trading ports of St. Michael's Mount (serving the continent), St. Ives and the Hayle estuary (whence it was exported to Wales and Ireland). The authenticity of Diodorus' records has been borne out by the discovery of a typical 'astragalus' ingot of tin, dredged up from the Fal estuary, obviously another important Iron Age port. It is a heavy H-shaped ingot nearly 3 feet (0.9m) long and can be seen in the County Museum in Truro.

The Cornish tin was taken by the Veneti to their home port of Corbilo on the southern coast of Brittany, and then on horseback down the west coast of France, through the Carcassone Gap to the Greek colony of Massilia where it was traded to merchants from the Mediterranean countries.

This happy state of affairs lasted until 56 BC, when Julius Caesar arrived in Brittany. His naval fleet fought a vicious battle in the Bay of Quiberon against the Veneti fleet which, in all probability, included Cornish ships. The leather-sailed Celtic ships, held in great respect by the Romans, were large, heavily-built oaken vessels with high poops and foredecks, well suited to Atlantic conditions. They stood much higher than Caesar's galleys, and so were difficult to board, and under sail were more manoeuvrable. However, at this battle disaster struck the Celts. The wind dropped. Unlike the Roman galleys, the Celtic ships were not equipped with banks of oars, so there they lay, helpless. Their fleet was routed and the survivors fled. By the close of the first century BC, many of the Celts in Cornwall were refugees from Brittany and it may well have been these people who introduced the elaborate and unusual courtyard houses and fogous.

Caesar's Gaulish campaigns prompted him to try to add Britain to his list of conquests. But, as history tells us, he was beaten off and it was left to Claudius and Vespasian to invade Britain. From AD 43 until AD 410, the Romans ruled much of the eastern and southern parts of the island, but they made little impression on the Cornish. They built a few small forts in the eastern half of Cornwall, abandoning them after only a few years. The nearest city was Exeter (Isca Dumnoniorum), separated from Cornwall by the inhospitable massif of Dartmoor. The only Romans the people of Belerion were likely to have seen were the occasional trader or teacher. For them, the Iron Age went on until the end of the fourth century AD. By then, the hut circle and courtyard house villages were being abandoned and new settlements were founded on lower ground; many of them to develop into the villages and towns of today. Another change had overcome the Celts of Cornwall – Christianity had arrived, spreading slowly during the later years of the Roman occupation.

The popular image of the Iron Age Celts as 'savage, primitive, woad-painted Ancient Britons' is fast fading, and rightly so. The study of contemporary records and of the remains of their civilisation shows that they were an advanced, tenacious and hard-working people.

One fine monument is their language. The Iron Age people of Brittany and mainland Britain spoke Brythonic (British), a branch of the Celtic tongue which later developed into Cornish, Welsh and Breton. The vast majority of place-names in west Cornwall are derived from Cornish, as will be seen later in this book.

Iron Age field monuments in West Penwith consist of six types. Taking the defensive sites first, there are the *hill forts*, which, as the name suggests, were fortified hilltops. The Land's End hill forts are relatively small, either round or oval, and their defences range from a single rampart with outer ditch to as many as four concentric banks and ditches. The walls or ramparts of these forts are of earth or stone, or both. Most had water supplies within the defences and, sometimes, traces of dwellings (usually hut circles) can still be seen.

Cliff castles are not crumbling, mysterious ruins of dark, clifftop towers like the Norman castle at Tintagel. They are similar to the hill forts, with from one to four banks and ditches protecting the landward approach to a prominent headland. The sea-cliffs provided adequate defence from every other direction. The oldest yet found is Maen Castle, between Sennen Cove and Land's End, which was built before 300 BC. It may well have been there when Pytheas paid his visit. Only a few cliff castles appear to have been permanently occupied; it seems that they were largely for refuge in case of invasion or similar trouble.

Another type of defensive site found in the Land's End peninsula is the *round*. Smaller than the hill forts and generally with only a single line of defence, most of these were walls defending a homestead, farm or village.

There were two kinds of Iron Age dwelling in West Penwith. First was the *hut circle*, which had appeared during the middle Bronze Age. In Penwith, hut circles were built of stone and, to begin with, were of the single-walled type; but, as building techniques improved, the double-walled hut became usual. This 'double' wall consisted of inner and outer stone facings with an earth or rubble infill. A hut circle might be anything from 9ft (2.7m) to 50ft (15.2m) in diameter, and was covered by a high, conical roof of thatch or turf. Many were found to have underfloor drainage, paved floors and central hearths.

During the first century BC, there developed in the Land's End peninsula the idea of including living quarters, workshops, stores and stables within a single building. This gave rise to the *courtyard house*. Strangely, these are found only in West Penwith; for some reason they did not spread to the rest of Cornwall. They were vastly superior to the hut circles and probably the wealthier farmers and tinners lived in them. It has been suggested that the design of the courtyard house was influenced by Roman buildings, but in fact the first ones were built before the Romans came to Britain.

A courtyard house is a massive structure, oval in plan and as much as 100ft (30.5m) long. The entrance, often facing away from the prevailing south-westerly winds, opens into a central, open courtyard. On one side there is usually a long recess which would have had a lean-to roof and was probably a stable or byre. On the opposite side there is often a long, oval room; and opposite the entrance, across the courtyard, is the large, round living room. All these are partly built into the thickness of the huge surrounding wall. These features are virtual constants, but the plan of each house and the number of rooms, up to as many as seven, varied according to the needs of its builder. The courtyard and entrances were paved with flat stones and each house had stone-lined and -covered drains. In excavated houses, hearths have been found; and in the main living room or 'round room', a large slab with a round socket cut into it to hold the base of the main roof support. These rooms had conical turf or thatch roofs.

More than two dozen courtyard house settlements still exist, ranging from single houses to the famous village of Chysauster, where there are at least eleven houses. Other features of these villages include conventional hut circles, garden plots and adjacent field systems, a feature also common to hut circle settlements.

A number of courtyard house villages include the strange structures known as *fogous*, deriving from the Cornish *fogo*, a cave. These are among the most fascinating of Cornwall's prehistoric buildings. They are stone-walled and -roofed passages, some underground, some semi-underground and one or two above ground. Most are curved, with corbelled walls, and many have side passages, some of which, negotiable only on hands and knees, are known aptly as 'creeps'. Their purpose is a complete mystery. Theories abound: they might be hidey-holes, escape routes, storage chambers, religious shrines or a combination of these. But each theory has a loophole and, although a number have been thoroughly excavated, the enigmatic fogou keeps its secrets. All were associated with either courtyard house villages or small fortified homesteads of the late Iron Age, and are found only west of the River Fal. They resemble the souterrains of Brittany, Ireland and Scotland.

The list that follows includes the best and most impressive of the Iron Age sites.

41 Bartinnê Castle, (?) Hill Fort, Crows-an-Wra.

NG 395293. *Marked as:* **Bartine Castle.**
Best reached by track opposite car park at foot of Chapel Cam Brea (see Site 4 for directions), then bear over open moor to hilltop, keeping disused china clay works to the right.

On the summit of the hill is a circular area 246ft (75m) across, marked out by a low bank of earth and scattered stones, which is nowhere more than 3ft (0.9m) high. A shallow encircling ditch has virtually disappeared.

In the centre of the enclosure are three small circular banks of earth and gravel arranged in a tight triangular plan: the edges of two actually join. There is no sign of the 'contiguous stones pitched on end' mentioned by Dr. Borlase. The largest and best preserved of these circles, now containing the Ordnance Survey triangulation pillar, is 39ft (11.8m) in diameter; the others are 26ft (7.9m) and 30ft (9.1m) across. Whether they are the remains of hut circles or ring barrows is not yet known.

What Bartinnê Castle actually was is also a mystery. Even though the enclosing bank has been extensively robbed, it seems that it was never strong enough to have been of any defensive value. Perhaps, as Dr. Borlase suggested, it was a hill fort, traced out, begun, but never finished. It could be that an alternative site was found at Caer Brân *(Site 48)* on the next hill. Another suggestion is that Bartinnê may have been a huge disc-barrow.

A third theory could be formed from a tradition heard by J.O. Halliwell and repeated in his *Rambles in Western Cornwall*. This held that the bank was formerly higher, with its inner slope fashioned into rows of rough seating, similar to the mediaeval Cornish Plên-an-gwarys. If this was not the result of a later re-use of the site, the possibility exists that Bartinnê was a sacred enclosure; indeed, legend tells us that no evil spirit can enter it. Fires were lit during the worship of the Celtic sun-god Belenos and it is worth noting that the name Bartinnê has been interpreted as deriving from the Cornish *bre tanow* — hill of fires.

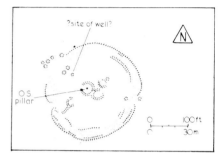

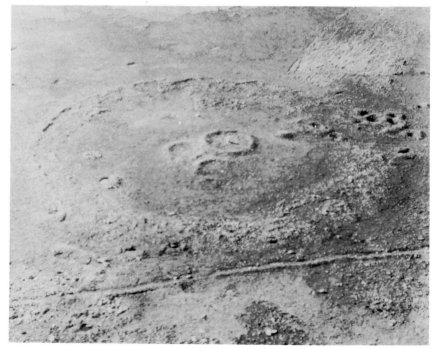

42 Bodrifty Hut Circle Settlement, New Mill.

NG 445354. *Marked as:* **settlement**.
Lane from New Mill leads NW to Bodrifty Farm. The site lies just to the N on edge of moorland.

A large and important settlement lying at the western foot of Mulfra Hill. Originally founded during the late Bronze Age, Bodrifty has the remains of a low surrounding bank of earth and stone enclosing roughly 3 acres (1.2ha), within which are seven well preserved hut circles, with walls up to 5ft (1.5m) high, and traces of at least three more. These huts, which average 30ft (9.1m) in diameter, consist of well-laid outer and inner facings with an infill of rubble. Most were found to have central hearths and stone drains, and many tall jambstones are still standing.

Excavations here by the West Cornwall Field Club from 1951 to 1955 revealed that Bodrifty was occupied continuously from the late Bronze Age to the late Iron Age, and no less than 3,000 sherds of pottery were turned up. Some huts, including the largest, were rebuilt in the Iron Age on Bronze Age foundations. Within this largest hut, situated towards the eastern side of the village, was a ring of post-holes, the sockets for the roof supports.

The bank surrounding the village, now no more than 3ft (0.9m) high, was an Iron Age addition. It can now be traced only around the northern side of the settlement, the rest having been obliterated by later field clearance and hedge building. The entrance, still visible, was on the south-west side. The area enclosed by this bank, which does not appear to have been defensive, was oval; 450ft (137m) from north-east to south-west, by 320ft (97m).

Immediately to the north-west of the enclosure are the low remains of a small hut circle, and another can be seen on the western side of a hedge about 300ft (91m) to the north. A third is traceable about 200ft (61m) east of the village, and is surrounded by the remains of a large field system.

At the time of writing, Bodrifty is a little difficult to observe owing to the growth of gorse. However, to the determined, it is well worth a visit and its importance forbids exclusion.

43 Boleigh Fogou, St. Buryan.

NG 437252. *Marked as:* **fogou**.
In private grounds of Rosemerrin House, the driveway to which leads off B3315 near the top of the hill on S side of Lamorna valley. Permission to visit must be sought from the occupier.

Boleigh Fogou (43)

This very impressive fogou pierced one of the ramparts of an Iron Age round which has virtually vanished since the building of Rosemerrin House during the 1920s. This round, which probably had two concentric ramparts, originally measured 140ft (43m) by 80ft (24m).

The fogou itself is beautifully preserved with a main gallery 36ft (10.9m) long and over 6ft (1.8m) high, entered from the south-west and curving slightly. On the west side of this gallery, near the entrance, is a small, well built portal leading into an L-shaped creep passage, at the innermost end of which is an unexplained false doorway. One of the lintels of this passage has fallen, leaving an open hole in the roof.

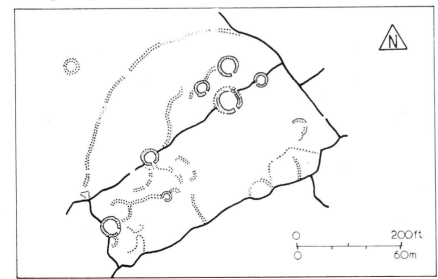

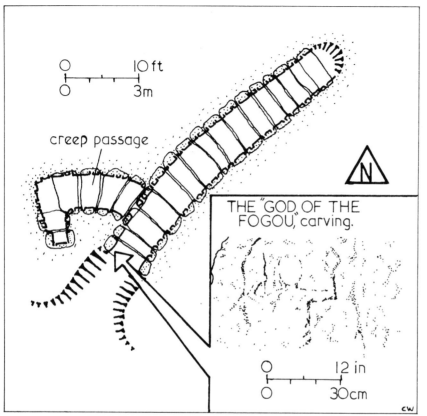

10ft

3m

creep passage

N

THE "GOD OF THE FOGOU" carving.

12 in

30cm

NG 417369. Marked as: Bosigran Castle. Reached by footpath N from B3306 just E of the Climbing Club, which stands beside prominent mine buildings 1½ miles NE of Morvah.

Positioned on one of Penwith's highest and most spectacular headlands, Bosigran Castle is the simplest example of its type. The single line of defence is a thick and well constructed wall drawn across the headland and taking advantage of a slight ridge. There is no external ditch.

The wall survives to a height of 5ft (1.5m) and had a central gateway, the blocked remains of which can still be seen just west of where a more recent wall joins the defensive work. There are no huts in the interior, but there may well have been a close connection between the cliff castle and two nearby courtyard house villages to be found in farm fields to the east.

The nearest of these, 500yds (460m) away and centred at NG 422371, consists of three, possibly four, courtyard houses, two of which are

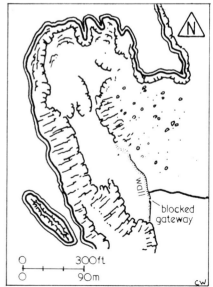

N

WALL

blocked gateway

300ft

90m

The fogou had only one entrance, the western jamb of which bears what appears to be an ancient and possibly unfinished carving in bas-relief. The upper part of a human figure is traceable, with upraised arms, one carrying a staff or spear, the other holding up a diamond shaped object which may be the head of a snake with its tail wrapped around the bearer's wrist. Whether this stone was brought from elsewhere when the fogou was built, or it was carved where it stands is not known, but it is possible that the figure is that of a Celtic god. If so, it would be one of the few such carvings in existence and may point to a possible religious use of this particular fogou.

The fogou was certainly never any longer than it is now, the inner end being hewn out of solid rock (unfortunately, the last lintel is missing), despite the former local belief that it stretched for miles. The local population once kept well away from the 'fogie hole', for they believed that devils and witches held their revels there. Nevertheless, during the Civil War, a party of fugitive Royalists swallowed their fear and successfully hid in the fogou from pursuing Roundhead troops.

The Boleigh fogou was excavated in 1945 by Dr. E.B. Ford and Mrs E. Clark, but it refused to reveal any of its secrets.

reasonably well preserved although nothing remains above a height of 4ft (1.2m). A remarkable circular cove of unknown date is built into the corner of a field beside one of these houses.

The second village, at NG 428370, lies just to the east of Bosigran Farm, where a single courtyard house was built against a north-facing terrace, now topped by a modern wall. Just to the south are the possible remains of another, mutilated by fairly recent stone structures known locally as 'crows' (Cornish: crow – hut). This building stands against the northern side of an excellent round 90ft (27m) across, with a massive wall up to 20ft (6.1m) thick, the southern side of which is now missing.

All these sites are now under the guardianship of the National Trust and none has yet been excavated.

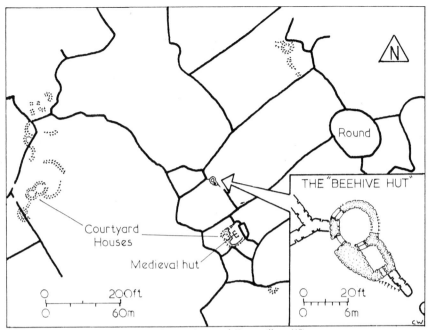

The scattered settlement of the Bosporthennis Courtyard House village (45)

45 Bosporthennis Courtyard House Village, Treen (North).

NG 438360. *Marked as:* **settlement**.
In fields 400yds (366m) SW of Bosporthennis (pronounced: Bosprenis) Farm, off Penzance – Gurnard's Head road 1 mile S of Treen.

The scattered remains of what must have been an extremely large settlement lie in the foot of the secluded valley at the eastern foot of Hannibal's Carn.

The most famous structure here is the so-called Beehive Hut, which is centrally placed within the settlement. This is a remarkable structure in the corner of a field and consists of a round, corbelled chamber 13ft (4.0m) across, connected to a rectangular room, 11ft by 7ft (3.3m by 2.1m), by a low but massive doorway. The end wall of the rectangular room, which contains a small window, is believed to be modern, as is the tall, lintelled south-western entrance to the round chamber. The walls of this building still reach a height of 7½ft (2.3m). It is not known for certain what the Beehive Hut actually was, but comparing its round chamber with the underground one at Carn Euny *(Site 50)*,

some people believe it to be a unique form of above-ground fogou.

The best of the courtyard houses lies 250yds (230m) to the west. Facing north-east, it appears to have only a courtyard and a round room, which has a back door. The entrances to courtyard and round room both have one jamb still standing, and the walls stand as high as 5ft (1.5m). A walled compound adjoins this house on the eastern side and fragments of at least three other buildings, possibly including another courtyard house, lie close by.

Another courtyard house lies just south of the Beehive Hut and is an example of a prehistoric building adapted for mediaeval use. The round room and courtyard are defined by walls up to 5½ft (1.6m) high and within the courtyard are the remains of a two-roomed mediaeval building with drystone walls 4ft (1.2m) high. A faint hut circle is also visible against the south side of a hedge nearby to the south-east.

To the north-west of the Beehive Hut is a round, defined by heavy walling, north of which is another ruinous feature which may be the remains of yet another courtyard house. Nearly the whole of this settlement now lies within farmland and many of the modern field walls are built on top of ancient terracing. The site is unexcavated.

46 Bosullow Trehyllys Courtyard House Village, Morvah.

NG 406342. Marked as: **settlement.**
From car park at Trehyllys Farm (see directions for Chûn Castle, Site 54) a track leads around the eastern base of the hill to a barely used lane between fields. The site lies on the right at the end of the lane.

In terms of preservation, this village is second only to the famous Chysauster *(Site 55)*, despite being unexcavated (that is apart from two examinations of a couple of rooms last century).

Overshadowed by the hill fort of Chûn Castle, the village is a closely-knit collection of at least five courtyard houses and fourteen hut circles, three of which are in the adjoining croft to the west. One of these has a large corral attached to it. Many of the hut circles form an interlocking complex on the eastern side of the village, reminiscent of Carn Euny *(Site 50)*. This complex also incorporates one of the courtyard houses, a fine example with walls 5ft (1.5m) high.

Three courtyard houses lie in a north-south line, the northerly pair of which are the best preserved with walls over 6ft (1.8m) high in places. The northern house appears to have two round rooms, the southernmost of the two was probably added later as the family increased. This house was partly cut into the gentle slope and both jambstones of the east-facing entrance still stand.

The central house seems to have been designed for two families. Both sides of the house have a long room, a round room with back door and with a small round room leading off, all spaced around a small, communal courtyard. Many jambstones survive, including one prominent 6ft (1.8m) example at the entrance to the house.

The southern house is unusual in that it has two courtyards. With no wall higher than 4ft (1.2m) it is the least well preserved of the three.

The remains of a fifth house lie in a field on the opposite side of the old lane on the north side of the village. Only its northern side is left, but signs of a long room can be seen within the stone mound which, in recent times, appears to have been a convenient dump for field clearance. Also in this field is a deep, narrow well, edged with large stones, which may be as old as the village; a saddle quern was found in it.

Around and amongst the buildings of this village are a number of tiny fields, paddocks and corrals, their boundaries visible as stony banks. The virtually disused lane passing the north side of the village is a remaining portion of the prehistoric trackway known locally as the 'Old St. Ives Road', and connects the village with Chûn Castle. Some have reported this trackway to be paved, but this is probably a mistaken interpretation of the flat natural boulders on the hillside. However, the trackway is slightly sunk into the ground to form a 'hollow way'.

The author has recently found what appears to be the roofless remains of an above-ground fogou, with a small, roofed creep passage, within this village.

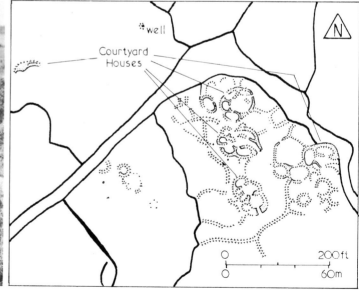

47 Boswarva Courtyard House Village, Madron.

NG 429330. *Not marked.*
Reached either by path from Penzance – Morvah road 300yds (274m) SE of Lanyon Quoit (Site 6), past Boswarva Carn, or by track from Boswarva Farm on Newbridge to Madron lane.

This settlement is not well known and is somewhat overgrown, but it is fairly large, with three courtyard houses and four hut circles set on south-west facing terraces.

The westernmost courtyard house may have been a semi-detached house, similar to House 3 at Chysauster *(Site 55)*, although little remains of its northern half. The southern half, with courtyard, round room and at least three other rooms, has walls as high as 4ft (1.2m) as does a single house south-east of it. Here again, its north side is poorly preserved, but courtyard, round room and a long room can be seen. Both houses have east-facing entrances.

The third house, on the north-eastern side of the settlement, is the largest known courtyard house, measuring 120ft (36.6m) by 100ft (30.5m), with walls up to 6ft (1.8m) high. Entered from the south-east, surprisingly it has only three rooms leading off the large courtyard.

Of the four hut circles, one is double-roomed and another, well preserved and with 6ft (1.8m) high walls, has a garden terrace adjoining its southern side.

48 Caer Brân Hill Fort, Sancreed.

NG 408290. *Marked as:* **Caer Brân.**
Reached by paths leading uphill from Carn Euny (Site 50) or S from St. Just to Sancreed road at Grumbla.

The superb hill fort of Caer Brân (Cornish: *Ker bran* – Fort Crow), 430ft (131m) in diameter, is set on the summit of Brane Hill with fine views in all directions.

There are two concentric lines of defence, the outermost being an earth rampart fronted by a wide ditch. These are best seen on the north side where the rampart rears as much as 15ft (4.6m) above the foot of the 7ft (2.1m) deep ditch, which still has signs of stone

revetment and a slight counterscarp bank along its outer edge. On the south-west side of the fort, above a disused roadstone quarry, both rampart and ditch are in poorer condition, becoming much slighter and broken by frequent gaps. In one place, the rampart ends are somewhat out of alignment, suggesting that the fort is unfinished.

Strangely, the 1908 Ordnance Survey map and Dr. Borlase's seventeenth-century sketch show the fort as perfect, although Borlase's

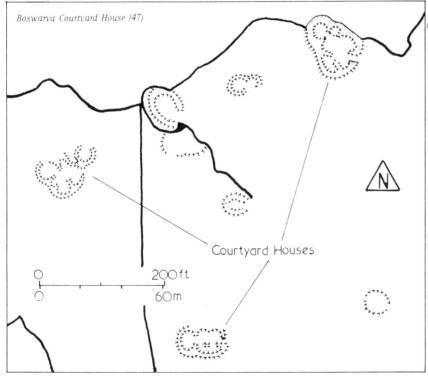

Boswarva Courtyard House (47)

Courtyard Houses

0   200ft

0   60m

drawing showed no entrances whatsoever and should be considered unreliable.

The original outer entrance is probably that facing north-west, where the causeway over the ditch is well defined and the butt-ends of the rampart show signs of having been stone-lined. This entrance is also closest to the ancient Penzance to Land's End trackway.

Within the outer rampart are the very shallow, much silted remains of an inner ditch and, set back from it, is what is left of the inner rampart. This was an earth bank, faced with stone, but the robbers have been here and very little stone is left. Much of this rampart has disintegrated leaving only four short stretches of bank between 3 and 6ft

(0.9m and 1.8m) high. It was originally about 15ft (4.6m) thick.

In the centre of the fort are the overgrown foundations of a large hut circle 52ft (15.8m) across. A disused but recent track cuts straight through it so that the position of its entrance cannot be determined without excavation, which has yet to take place at this site.

Caer Brân overlooked at least three Iron Age settlements. The well-known Carn Euny *(Site 50)* is 400yds (366m) to the south-west; Goldherring *(Site 59)* is ½ mile to the south and there are scattered hut circles on the facing slope of Bartinney Hill, ½ mile to the west.

Just to the east of the fort is a small, pear-shaped round with a single bank 6ft (1.8m) high, in the centre of which are traces of a hut platform.

In local legend, Caer Brân is said to be a sanctuary from evil spirits and is also reputed to be a haunt of the elusive Small People.

49 Caergwidden Round, Newbridge.

NG 415310. *Marked as:* **enclosure.**
On S side of a track leading W to Derval Farm off lane from Newbridge to Sancreed.

On the southern slope of Trannack Hill is this fine, unexcavated round which, before the removal of its east side, measured 144ft (44m) by 110ft (34m). It is defined by a single stone wall up to 9ft (2.7m) high which, in places, shows traces of a parapet walk. The external ditch has been completely ploughed out. It is not certain where the original entrance was situated, but old reports state that it was roofed by a massive lintel.

The interior of the round is known to have contained a number of hut circles, but none now remain. A fogou is also thought to have existed here, but it is possible that this could have been a memory of the round's entrance.

Left: *Caer Brân hill fort (48).*
Below: *Plan and photograph of Caergwidden Round (49).*

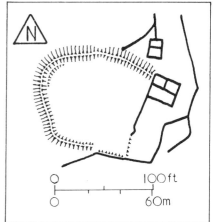

50 Carn Euny Courtyard House Village and Fogou, Sancreed. DE.

NG 402289. *Marked as:* **Carn Euny – settlement.**
Well signposted from A30 at Drift. A mile or so of narrow, tortuous lane has to be negotiated. Car park just beyond Brane Farm.

Excavated by Dr. V. Favell in 1927-8 and by the Ministry of Works from 1964 to 1970, this is a fascinating village consisting of an interlocking series of unusual courtyard houses in which the round room is missing; they seem to be a mixture of hut circle and courtyard house design. Four such houses are known here, the best being the most northerly pair. Both of these are roughly circular, 62ft (18.9m) across, containing a large courtyard with a long room on either side of the paved entrance. The entrances of these two houses face in opposite directions. Detached hut circles are also a feature of this settlement which, although well maintained, has no wall higher than 4½ft (1.3m).

These houses were built during the first century BC, replacing a series of timber huts built in the sixth century BC, and there were traces of activity dating back to neolithic times. These long-vanished timber huts had stone drainage channels and roof posts over 6in (15cm) thick, hewn from the trees which at that time grew quite thickly in this pocket of the hillside.

The occupants of Carn Euny were primarily farmers, but probably had a sideline in tin-streaming.

The most remarkable feature of this site is the magnificent fogou, the entrance to which is beside that of the most northerly courtyard house. Its slightly curving main gallery, 66ft (20m) long and over 6ft (1.8m) high, is open at both ends and was found to have had a paved floor with drainage channels. 42ft (12.8m) of this gallery is roofed.

From its west side, near the south-west exit, a tiny creep passage angles upward to the surface and, at the opposite end of the main gallery, also on the western side, is a low, short passage leading into an amazing corbelled chamber 15ft (4.6m) in diameter and 8ft (2.4m) high. It is completely below ground level, but the very top of its domed roof has gone. At the foot of the chamber's wall, opposite the entrance, is a curious recess resembling a flueless fireplace. This has not been explained.

At some time in the past, the fogou was deliberately filled in with earth and this probably contributed to its excellent preservation, although it must be said that part of the roof has been restored. It was cleared out last century and, following the recent excavations, is now accessible to all.

Both the village and the fogou are maintained by the Department of the Environment (and there is a small admission fee).

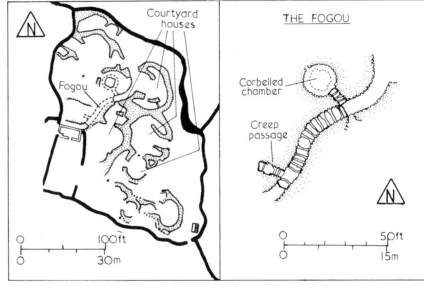

51 Carn Lês Boel, Cliff Castle, Sennen.

NG 357233. *Marked as:* **cliff castle.**
Reached by cliff path running S from Land's End which passes the site.

The central spine of this fine headland, on the southern side of Nanjisal Bay, is naturally defended by a prominent rock mass, but on its northern side, running down the steep coastal slope to the cliff edge, are two earth and stone ramparts, each with their external ditches.

The shallow outer ditch, 10ft (3.0m) wide, guards a weak rampart no more than 2½ft (0.8m) high, but behind this is a much stronger bank as high as 7ft (2.1m).

On the southern coastal slope is a stony, unditched bank which may well be artificial, and on the central ridge, which forms a natural causeway into the defended area, are two large stones, one fallen, the other standing 4ft (1.2m) tall. These were probably the jambstones of the vanished entrance.

To the east of these defences are signs of a faint bank and ditch which cut off the entire headland and may represent an unfinished outer line of defence.

This little-known cliff castle is unexcavated and no huts have been found on the headland.

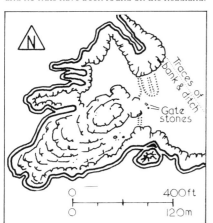

52 Castallack Roundago, Paul.

NG 448254. *Not marked.*
Reached by lane from B3315 at Sheffield to Lamorna, and turning right at Castallack Farm. The site is 250yds (230m) from the farm on the N side of the track.

This Iron Age round measures 180ft (55m) from east to west by 160ft (49m), and parts of its massive wall remain. Some parts of this wall, which is from 3ft to 6ft (0.9m to 1.8m) thick, consist of pillars up to 6ft tall with smaller stones crammed in between in rough courses. Other parts are constructed of huge blocks laid horizontally on each other, forming inner and outer facings with an infill of earth and stones.

Just outside the enclosure, to the north-west, are the remains of a hut circle; and a curious cupped stone can be seen in the wall on the western interior of the round.

The entrance to the Roundago was on the south side and a colonnade of erect stones once led from it to a circular hut near the centre of the round. Nothing now remains of either stones or hut.

Just to the west of the round, on Castallack Carn, is a small Bronze Age menhir, 6ft (1.8m) tall.

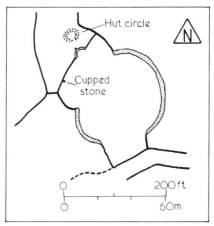

53 Castle-an-Dinas Hill Fort, Nancledra.

NG 485350. *Marked as:* **Castle-an-dinas.**
A footpath leaves the W side of B3311 at Castle Gate, skirting the W side of large quarry workings, and leads to the hilltop, where 'Rogers' Tower' acts as a useful landmark.

The name of this well-known but ruinous hill fort is tautologous, meaning nothing more than the 'castle castle'! It is one of two forts to bear this name, the other being near St. Columb Major.

435ft (133m) across, it originally had two massive, concentric stone walls, an earth and stone rampart beyond them and an outer rampart which reaches less than halfway around the fort. Traces remain, in places, of an outer ditch.

Of the inner wall, once 12ft (3.7m) thick, little remains, although its foundations can just be traced. 30ft (9.1m) beyond this are the ruins of the second wall, now a tumble of drystone blocks up to 5ft (1.5m) high with just a few glimpses of vertical facing visible.

A space of about 60ft (18.3m) separates this wall from the third line of defence which reaches a height of 7ft (2.1m), although at least half of it has been topped by modern field walls. The final and outermost defence, an earth rampart, seems to be an unfinished structure, but it is fairly massive, reaching 8ft (2.4m) in height, and fronted for much of its length by a shallow ditch.

The location of the fort's original entrance is not known. There are a number of breaches in its defences, including one well-defined opening in the outer rampart, with a causeway over the ditch and out-turned rampart ends. This may have been a false entrance to trap the unwary, for there are no corresponding gaps in the inner defences at this point. The north-western and south-eastern gaps, which break all the defences, appear to be recent.

In the centre of the fort, close to the Ordnance Survey pillar, are the foundations of a hut circle 24ft (7.0m) in diameter. If this is a hut, and there

are some doubts, then it is the only survivor of several noted by Dr Borlase, three of which are shown on Charles Henderson's plan drawn early this century.[*] A well, also described by Dr Borlase, has entirely disappeared.

As can be seen, Castle-an-dinas has suffered terribly over the centuries at the hands of stone-robbers. The erection, in 1798 of the folly known as Rogers' Tower was to some extent responsible for its dilapidated state as it was built of stone from the castle walls and stands in a gap forced through the second wall.

Among the Iron Age settlements under the protection of this fort was the famous Chysauster (Site 55), ¾ mile to the west.

The restless ghost of Wild Harris haunts this spot, having been put to task here by the once-famous ghost-layer, Parson Polkinghorne. The spectre must count the blades of grass within the inner enclosure nine times, reaching the same total each time, before being assured of peace.

[*]Two further huts were found in the interior of the fort by the author, in 1985.

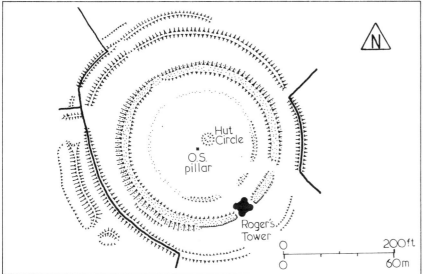

Left: *Castle-an-Dinas hill fort (53)*

43

54 Chûn Castle, Hill Fort, Morvah.

NG 405339. *Marked as:* **Chûn Castle**.
A lane, signposted 'Chûn Castle' leads W from the Penzance – Morvah road at Bosullow Common, 1 mile SE of Morvah. Cars may be parked at Trehyllys Farm, whence a path, indicated by a whitewashed boulder, leads up to the hill top. The name is pronounced 'Choon'.

Chûn Castle (Cornish: *Chy wun* – house on the downs) stands on a lonely moorland hilltop and, despite its ruinous state, is extremely impressive. Built during the third century BC, it differs from most of its fellow hill forts in that it was constructed entirely of stone.

280ft (85m) in diameter, its defences consisted of two concentric granite walls with external rock-cut ditches. The outer ditch was 20ft (6.1m) wide and perhaps 4ft (1.2m) deep, but what little remains of it is now choked, shallow and ill-defined.

The outer wall is, on average, 6½ft (2.0m)

thick and, on the outside, is as much as 7ft (2.1m) high, although in one or two places it has been virtually destroyed. An earthen ramp backing the wall sloped down into the inner ditch, which is no longer evident as such.

About 30ft (9.1m) within the outer wall stands the ruin of the once-massive inner wall, now tumbled into a circular heap of stone from 5ft to 8ft (1.5m to 2.4m) high. Some of its original outer facing, built with a slight inward batter for stability, is still visible, the best example being an 80ft (24m) length south of the inner entrance. The thickness of the wall is astounding; 15ft (4.6m) for the most part, but gradually widening to 22ft (6.7m) on either side of the tapering, bottlenecked gateway, which still has its tall, massive gateposts.

Once, the outer wall stood 10ft (3.0m) or more in height; the inner perhaps as much as 20ft (6.1m), but over the last few centuries the castle has suffered horribly, much of its stone being taken to build the now demolished Madron Workhouse and to pave some of the streets of Penzance.

On the northern side of the inner courtyard is a stone-lined well, which still holds water. It is known to be 12ft (3.7m) deep, but it is somewhat choked by loose stone which some individuals insist on throwing in, despite the efforts of the author and others to keep it clear.

From around the time of Christ, Chûn Castle fell into comparative disuse until the sixth century AD, when it was reoccupied and underwent certain modifications. The new lords of the castle built fifteen or sixteen stone houses around the inner courtyard and backing onto the inside of the great wall. The sub-rectangular foundations of these can still be seen, some overlying the sites of circular Iron Age huts. In one of these houses was found the typical 'grass marked' pottery of the south-western Dark Age, and in another was a 12lb (5.44kg) lump of tin slag. Excavators also found an elaborate smelting furnace just south of the well, although nothing is visible there now.

Also during this Dark Age phase, or so it appears, the castle entrance was ingeniously redesigned. The original outer gate, the stones

Left: *Reconstruction of Chûn Castle (54) as it might have appeared during its final occupation.*

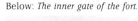
Opposite: *Aerial photograph and plan of Chûn Castle.*

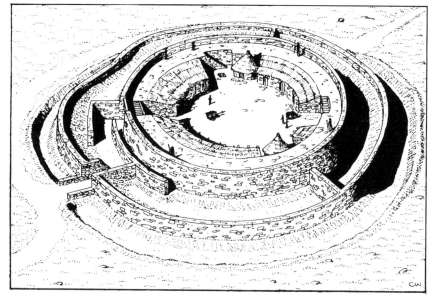

Below: *The inner gate of the fort.*

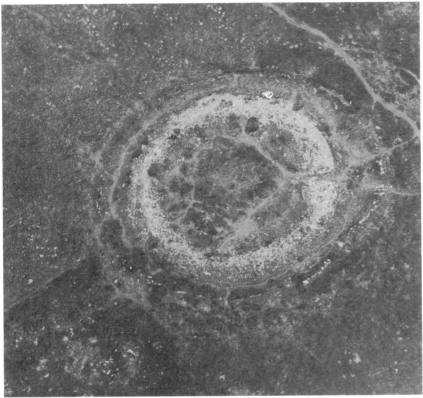

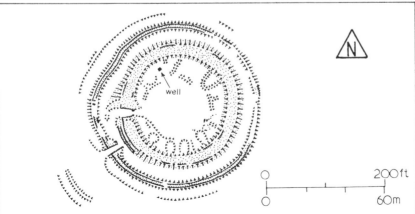

of which can still be seen opposite the inner gateway, was blocked up and another built some way to the south of it. This, with a series of curtain and transverse walls, produced a staggered entry which would force any unwanted intruder to negotiate a narrow, twisting passage that exposed his shieldless right side to the castle's defenders on the inner wall.

Outside this later outer gateway are the faint remains of a length of bank and ditch, probably designed to break up any concentrated assault on the gate.

A number of Iron Age fortresses in the south west were similarly reoccupied and modified, probably as a safeguard against barbarian attack from the sea.

Chûn Castle was probably built to protect the precious tin, which was mined and streamed locally. The tin ore, lifeblood of the early economy of Penwith, was brought here for storage and smelting before being taken on to the trading ports at the Hayle estuary and St. Michael's Mount. Once within the massive walls of Chûn, it would certainly have been safe, for the castle must have been virtually impregnable.

The fort stands astride the route of the prehistoric trackway known as the 'Old St. Ives Road', which, on the north-east side of the hill, shows as a slightly sunken way before becoming a narrow lane between fields. Here, at the base of the hill, are the extensive remains of Bosullow Trehyllys (Site 46), a superb courtyard house village. There are two other, smaller settlements within 1/2 mile of the castle: Crofto (Site 57) and Carn House, both lying to the north.

Small excavations took place at Chûn Castle in 1862 and 1895, but the most important were a series of digs carried out by E. Thurlow Leeds in 1925, 1927 and 1930.

Legend provides one of those curious links with archaeological fact. According to the old stories, the builder of Chûn Castle was a curious character known as Jack of the Hammer, or Jack the Tinner, a wandering tin prospector and cunning lore-master who settled in Penwith. He was also the original giant-killer.

55 Chysauster Courtyard House Village, New Mill. DE.

NG 472350. Marked as: **Chysauster – settlement.** *The site is well signposted and reached by the back lane to New Mill which leaves B3311 at Badger's Cross. A footpath leads to the site from the car park.*

Chysauster is a classic site, the largest of the courtyard house villages and one of the finest prehistoric villages to be found anywhere in Britain.

Eight houses form two rows of four with a winding village street between. Most of them have a terraced garden plot attached and house 3 is a semi-detached dwelling, the northern unit of which was added to a formerly single house. In each case, the entrance to the house faces away from the prevailing south-westerly wind. A ninth house stands by the custodian's hut (from which a fine guide can be purchased) and traces of two more lie in a field to the west.

Houses 4 and 6 are virtually perfect, lacking only the conical thatch or turf roofs to their round living rooms (where, in houses 3 and 6, there is a narrow back door) and the lean-to roofs of the workshops, storerooms and stables. Admittedly, some restoration has been done, but the walls of these two houses are over 6ft (1.8m) high; one wall in house 6 is 7½ft (2.3m) high. House 6 is also the most elaborate, with no less than seven rooms surrounding the courtyard.

Stone-covered drains are still visible in four of the houses and the socketed stone that held the main roof-support post can be seen in a number of the round living rooms, which are always directly opposite the entrance to the house. Some rooms, doorways and entrances are paved with rough granite slabs.

It has been suggested by some that courtyard houses were native imitations of Roman dwellings, but it is clear that Chysauster was built before the Romans ever came to Britain, perhaps as early as 100 BC. There is no sign of any Roman influence; probably the only Romans to visit West Penwith were traders and the occasional teacher. The inhabitants of the village

were farmers and perhaps tinstreamers, and it is very likely that they were under the protection of the hill fort of Castle-an-dinas *(Site 53),* ¾ mile to the east. By 300 AD, the village was beginning to be gradually and peacefully abandoned.

For centuries, Chysauster lay overgrown and almost unknown, being referred to merely as the 'Crellas' (ruins), then as the 'Chapels' when the site was used by Methodist preachers in the early nineteenth century. It was not until 1849 that Chysauster was recognised for what it is. Since then, it has undergone extensive excavations. Three of the houses in the main body of the village, plus the outlying pair, have not yet been dug.

Chysauster stood in the midst of a vast field system which stretches for almost a mile along the hillside. Parts of this are easily traceable immediately to the north-east of the village, but much was destroyed to the north and north-west, by the landowner, in 1984.

Just to the south lie the rather disappointing remains of a fogou. Built underground, it is thought to have been about 50ft (15m) long, but now just 15ft (4.6m) is left, with only two massive roofing stones in place. It was excavated in the last century by W.C. Borlase.

Like most fogous, it has corbelled walls and the present headroom is only 4½ft (1.3m). The appearance of the ground to the east suggests that another structure, perhaps a second fogou or another house, once stood there.

Chysauster is beautifully maintained by the Department of the Environment and, as at Carn Euny, there is a small admission fee.

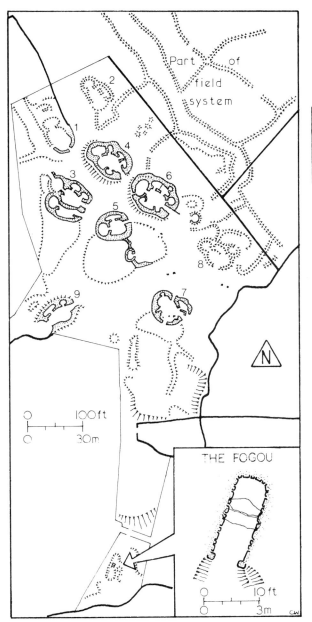

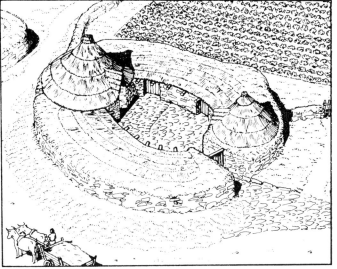

Above: *Reconstruction of House 6 in the Chysauster settlement (55).*
Left: *Plan of the settlement.*
Opposite: *Aerial photograph of the settlement.*

47

56 Crankan Courtyard House Village, New Mill.

NG 461343. *Not marked.*
Access by path from New Mill – Chysauster road 200 yds (183m) from its junction with Penzance – Gurnard's Head road.

This overgrown settlement of courtyard houses and hut circles is large and scattered amongst an extensive field system, but the two courtyard houses, linked by a modern wall, are quite close to one another.

The north-eastern house is not easily recognisable as such, but takes the form of a near-circular enclosure with a partly-modern surrounding wall up to 6½ft (2.0m) high. The interior, sunk about 3ft (0.9m) below the top of the wall, has a depression on the north-eastern side which probably represents the courtyard. Only the faintest of traces of other rooms can be seen.

The south-western house is better defined, with walls 4ft (1.2m) high. The south-east facing entrance still has its north jambstone standing and the remains of a long room and a smaller chamber can be seen on the southern side of the courtyard. The round room, however, is only just traceable. Around the east side of the house, enclosed by a wall, is a long, curving, sunken feature looking suspiciously like an above ground fogou, at the inner end of which is a modern shelter built into the wall of the courtyard house.

Just west of this house are the ruins of a round, now on the lip of a deep, disused quarry. Its northern half is defined by a modern wall, but the foundations of ancient walling can be seen around the southern side with a possible entrance facing the courtyard house.

To the north, east and south of the courtyard houses are a number of scattered hut circles and also, to the south at NG 460340, are the remains of a mediaeval longhouse 52ft (15.8m) long by 11ft (3.3m) wide.

Among rocks some 150yds (137m) east of the longhouse, at NG 462340, is the curious 'Giant's House', probably a seventeenth century cottage partly built into the rocks, which is believed to stand on the site of a late Bronze Age dwelling.

Crankan Courtyard House

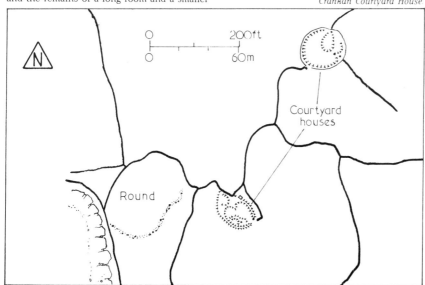

57 Crofto Courtyard House Village, Morvah.

NG 403349. *Not marked.*
Reached by a muddy path SE from B3306 at NG 398351, keeping to left of stream.

In a small, uncultivated field beside the spring, Crofto stands in the shallowest of valleys. It consists of three courtyard houses, two of them unusually elaborate and somewhat unconventional. Mutilation by stone robbing and earth infilling has been rife here and the only excavation undertaken was of a long chamber in the north-western house. This chamber is the only one in the village still to show extensive walling.

This house was entered from the south, where a large jambstone can be seen, with the excavated chamber to the right, then another narrow entrance leads into the courtyard which has two circular rooms leading off. The walls are generally low, but reach 5½ft (1.6m) in the long chamber, which is somewhat fogou-like.

The north-eastern house appears to be a semi-detached dwelling. The western unit, entered from the south-west, is fairly conventional, with a round room, a smaller circular room and a fragmentary long room. The eastern side is much smaller and more difficult to make out, but it appears to have a tiny courtyard with

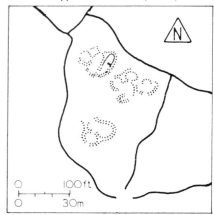

two round chambers opening into it. No wall in this house is higher than 2ft (0.6m).

The third house, to the south of its neighbours, has a courtyard, round room and two side chambers, but the position of its entrance is not certain. The walls here reach a height of 3½ft (1.1m).

58 Faugan Round, Hill Fort, Newlyn.

NG 452282. *Marked as:* **Faugan**.
On W side of footpath between Rose Farm, on the Drift – Chywoone Grove road, and Tredavoe.

Greatly damaged by agriculture over the centuries, this hill fort, with extensive views over Mount's Bay, shows the remains of two concentric ramparts. These are spaced about 100ft (30.5m) apart and are topped by modern field walls for much of their length. The inner rampart still reaches a height of 6½ft (2.0m), but large parts of the outer bank are missing. The ditches, too, have been ploughed out.

On the eastern side of the inner enclosure are two upright stones 5½ft and 6ft (1.7m and 1.8m) high and standing 9ft (2.7m) apart. Known as the Stones Faugan, these are the gateposts of the long vanished inner entrance to the fort.

No excavations have taken place at this hill fort, which was 400ft (122m) in diameter.

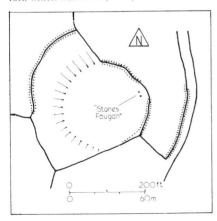

59 Goldherring Courtyard House Settlement, Sancreed.

NG 411282. *Marked as:* **settlement**.
Reached by track leading N from A30 just W of entrance to Goldherring Farm.

The large, uncultivated field in which this settlement is situated is filled with the clear traces of a prehistoric field system which, at one point, is crossed by a mediaeval wall. The settlement itself is in the north-eastern corner of the field and is surrounded by a round measuring 140ft (43m) from west to east by 120ft (37m). The single wall of this round now reaches a height of 5ft (1.5m) and parts of a shallow ditch can be seen. A fine, paved entrance faces east.

Excavations within the round, by the West Cornwall Field Club from 1958 to 1962 uncovered the remains of a single courtyard house, hut circles and the site of a destroyed well. Another ancient well exists just to the east of the site. The courtyard house, with round room, two long rooms and a small oval chamber was partly overlaid by later oval and rectangular structures. One of these, on the eastern side of the round, was used possibly in the Dark Age and certainly in the early mediaeval period, as a tin-smelting site.

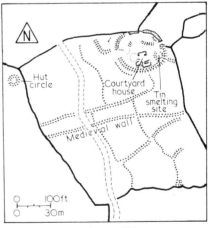

Goldherring Courtyard House (59)

Left & top of page: The hill fort, Faugan Round (58)

60 Gurnard's Head Cliff Castle, Treen (North). NT.

NG 433385. *Marked as:* **Trereen Dinas**.
Reached by footpath running N from Treen.

The earliest name of this headland was Ynyal (desolate), and the name Trereen Dinas shown on the Ordnance Survey map, which refers to the Iron Age fortifications, must not be confused with the larger fort of Treryn Dinas *(Site 73)* on the south coast near Porthcurno.

Across the high, narrow neck of the headland are two ramparts and three ditches, excavated by the West Cornwall Field Club in 1939. The outermost ditch, some 30ft (9.1m) south of the main defences, is only extant on the eastern clifftop and has no backing rampart. It may be that this is an unfinished feature. It is 4ft (1.2m) deep and 9ft (2.7m) wide.

The remains of a shallow ditch lie in front of the stone and earth outer rampart, which is now no higher than 4ft (1.2m). Behind this was a rock-cut ditch 15ft (4.6m) wide.

The inner rampart, immediately behind this ditch, proved to be the most interesting feature of the site. Built of dry masonry, it is 17ft (5.2m) thick at the base and survives to a height of only 6ft (1.8m). Excavation found that the back of this rampart had been stepped to provide a stance for slingers, similar in design to a Breton cliff castle. The slingshot was a favourite long-range weapon of the Celts and, in their hands, was accurate and deadly.

An entrance gap breaks the centre of both ramparts and the two halves of each defence are slightly out of alignment, producing a twisting entry. The wearing down of the rampart ends by the much used footpath has now somewhat destroyed this effect.

There are at least sixteen hut circles to be found on the headland behind the defences. These are in two groups: 50 and 190yds (46m and 173m) north of the inner rampart. The huts are from 20 to 30ft (6.1m to 9.1m) in diameter and those which were excavated had central hearths, well-defined entrances and walls with inner and outer facings.

Below & above right: *Gurnard's Head cliff castle*

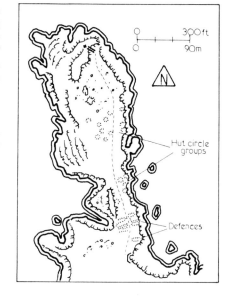

61 Kenidjack Castle, Cliff Castle, St. Just.

NG 356326. *Marked as:* **Kenidjack Castle**.
Lane W from B3306 in valley bottom just N of St. Just becomes a track leading to disused quarry on clifftop. The site lies just to N. immediately below ruined cottage and disused rifle-range butts.

The neck of the headland, with fine views of Cape Cornwall and Land's End to the south and Botallack mine to the north, is centrally protected by a natural, high rocky spine with traces of a defensive line across its landward end, but on the coastal slope on its northward side is a well-preserved triple fortification.

Behind an outer ditch 18ft (5.5m) wide and 3ft (0.9m) deep, are three sharp ramparts 8ft, 11ft and 7ft (2.4m, 3.3m and 2.1m) high. Although covered with grass, these banks are faced with stone and much of the inner rampart's masonry is now spread and exposed. A narrow entrance gap penetrates each bank at the foot of the central spine, leading to two hut circles further out on the headland.

The defences on the south side of the headland lie behind a natural rocky ridge and consist of two dilapidated ditches and banks, originally built of dry masonry but now no higher than 3ft (0.9m). Again, much of the inner bank's stone is exposed and, in one place, there is a small stretch of vertical facing. Tucked behind this rampart are two circular hut platforms.

There is some reason to believe that one of the major sources of prehistoric tin may have been in the Kenidjack valley and it is significant that the cave at its end (Porthledden) was guarded by a cliff castle on either side; one used to exist on Cape Cornwall.

Kenidjack Castle is also notable as being the source of the neolithic Group XVII axes. The site has not been excavated.

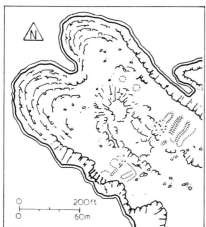

Above & top right: *Kenidjack Castle (61)*

Far right: *Kerris Roundago (62)*

62 Kerris Roundago, Round, Paul.

NG 445272. *Marked as:* **Roundago**.
Lane to Kerris leads W from B3315 1 mile S of Newlyn. Site lies 1 mile down this lane immediately behind converted chapel.

Although its western half has disappeared under the plough, this round originally measured 150ft (45.7m) from north to south, by 90ft (27.4m). A slight change in ground level indicates the site of the missing side.

Four rough pillars once formed an entrance rectangle 18ft (5.5m) long and 11ft (3.3m) wide at the southern end of the enclosure, but of these, only the southern pair remains. These are 6½ft (2.0m) and 6ft (1.8m) high and are incorporated into the wall.

The missing stones and much of the wall were removed in 1840 for the building of Penzance breakwater, and it is said that the workhorses employed in the destruction of the round, although young and healthy, died before the work was completed. This was taken to be a supernatural warning to those who would defile the works of the old ones.

200yds (183m) to the north of the round, at NG 444274, is a fine Bronze Age menhir. This is a great slab 7½ft (2.2m) high and 9ft (2.7m) across at the base, set on edge and roughly triangular in shape. W.C. Borlase, who dug here last century, found a pebble and a flint at its foot; a banded sandstone pendant has also been found here.

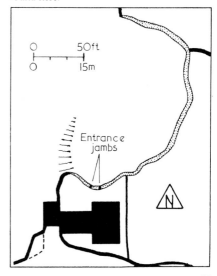

51

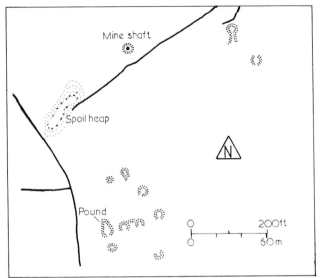

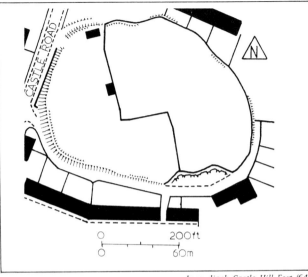

Lanyon Hut Circle settlement (63).

Lescudjack Castle Hill Fort (64).

63 Lanyon Hut Circle Settlement, Madron.*

NG 428344. *Not marked.*
Halfway along path from just S of Lanyon Farm, on Penzance – Morvah road, to the prominent engine house of Ding Dong Mine, then strike NW across the first piece of moorland. The site lies just in front of a disused mine tip. BEWARE OF MINE SHAFTS.

The main group of huts contains the remains of eight buildings averaging 20ft (6.1m) in diameter, with a triangular enclosure which may have been a livestock pound. The walls of these huts, although well-defined, are no higher than 2ft (0.6m) and all are of the single-walled type; i.e. of a single thickness of blocks, with the exception of one hut just south of the triangular pound which shows inner and outer facings.

500ft (152m) north-east of this group is another pair of huts, again, of the single-walled type, and both groups lie in the remains of a field system. No excavations have taken place at this site which, judging from the simplicity of the hut design, may date from the Bronze Age.

On the opposite side of the Lanyon – Ding Dong footpath, at NG 431342 and also on the fringe of the moor, are the remains of what appears to be a small neolithic Scillonian chamber tomb. The remains of a kerbed mound 21ft (6.4m) in diameter contains a roofless south-east facing chamber 5ft (1.5m) long and 2½ft (0.7m) wide, with a narrow entrance passage 2ft (0.6m) long. The mound now stands about 3½ft (1.1m) high.

*The 1984 excavation of this site may assign to it a date earlier than Iron Age.

64 Lescudjack Castle Hill Fort, Penzance.

NG 475310. *Not marked.*
Beside Castle Road, Penzance, at top of hill.

It is to the shame of Penzance that the hill fort of Lescudjack Castle, the oldest man-made structure in the town, has become the pitiful ruin it is today. It was once described as having had three lines of defence, but now shows only parts of a single rampart. The local historian Peter Pool has suggested that Hals' reference to triple defences may indicate that the entrance, now lost, had protective outworks. The position of the fort on the brink of a very steep slope makes it difficult to imagine triple ramparts and ditches completely surrounding it. The destruction of the fort is largely due to the building of a modern housing estate; now, half of its interior is used for allotments. Any surrounding ditch has utterly disappeared, but the remains of the rampart, on the south-western side, reach an external height of 16ft (4.9m). The ground level of the fort's interior was raised so that the highest part of the rampart there is only 2½ft (0.8m). Much of the outer face of the rampart alongside Castle Road is now obscured by an ugly concrete retaining wall.

Lescudjack Castle is the largest of the Land's End hill forts. It is oval in plan, measuring 500ft (152m) from west to east, by 400ft (122m). It is linked in legend with the Mên Scryfa inscribed stone *(Site 90)* which is a possible indication that it was occupied during the fifth or sixth century AD, at least 800 years after it was built.

65 Lesingey Round Hill Fort, Penzance.

NG 453304. *Marked as:* **Lesingey Round**.
*1 mile W of Penzance, reached by a lane between the
A3071 and the Tremethick Cross – Heamoor road.
Access through Lesingey Farm. The site is prominently
tree-covered.*

In contrast to the neighbouring Lescudjack
Castle *(Site 64)*, Lesingey Round is the smallest
of the Land's End hill forts, having an overall
diameter of just 260ft (79m). The single earth
rampart is quite massive and well preserved,
reaching a height of 12ft (3.7m) above the
surrounding ditch which, at the most, is 5ft
(1.5m) deep. The battered and somewhat ill-
defined entrance faces west. The interior of the
fort was raised above the surrounding ground
level and no traces of any huts have been found,
although excavation has yet to take place here.

It is not known for certain whether Lesingey

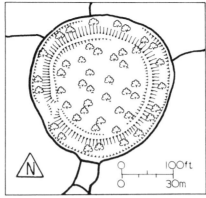

Lesingey Round (65).

Round (*lys an ke* – the hedged stronghold) is its
oldest name – the fort is surrounded by a
modern hedge – or whether the nearby house of
Castle Horneck (*hornek* – iron-like) took its name
from the fort.

66 Lower Boscaswell Fogou, Pendeen.

NG 377348. *Not marked.*
*Road to Lower Boscaswell leads NW from B3306 at
Pendeen. Two rough lanes lead from the village
towards the cliffs. The site lies off N side of the
southerly (left hand) lane after about 50yds (46m).*

This curious structure is built into a large and
ancient wall, which bulges to include a strange,
oval enclosure. The present entry into the fogou
is in a field on the north-western side of the
wall, and the length of the main passage as now
seen is just 8ft (2.4m), with a width of 6½ft
(1.9m). This was not the original entry to the
fogou, but a small creep passage can be seen. 4ft
(1.2m) long and 2ft (0.6m) wide, it opens into the
field just south of the present entrance, which
was the inner end of the fogou.

The original entrance to the main passage
was in the oval chamber and traces of foundations
found under the floor of the chamber indicate
that the fogou was at least 17ft (5.2m) long. The
end of the remaining length of passage was
blocked off in recent times.

It is not certain what function the oval
chamber served, although it is possible that it
may have been part of a courtyard house,
adapted in mediaeval times to become a garden.
The present dimensions of the chamber are 28ft
(8.5m) by 19ft (5.8m).

The site was excavated in 1954 by Mrs E.
Clark, Dr E.B. Ford and Charles Thomas.

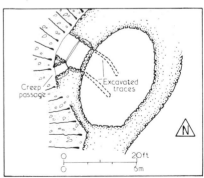

67 Maen Castle, Cliff Castle, Sennen. NT.

NG 348258. *Marked as:* **Maen Castle**.
Beside cliff path between Sennen Cove and Land's End.

Excavations by the West Cornwall Field Club in 1939 and 1948-9 revealed that Maen Castle (*men* is Cornish for stone) was built before 300 BC, making it the oldest known of the cliff castles.

The small, rocky headland was defended by a stone wall, ditch and counter-scarp bank. The ditch, dug to the very edge of the northern cliff, extends 190ft (58m) southwards and, at its northern end, there is a pronounced counter-

scarp revetted by heavy stone blocks and reaching 6ft (1.8m) in height on its outer side. The ditch is broad, U-shaped in section and from 3ft (0.9m) to 8ft (2.4m) deep.

The inner defence, separated from the ditch by a wide berm, is a wall 12ft (3.7m) thick, part of which was built by placing huge stones in an upright position forming parallel lines with the space between filled with rubble. The rest of the wall is of the more conventional coursed drystone. The narrow gateway is well preserved and constructed of massive blocks of granite. One of its former gate jambs, 8ft (2.4m) long, lies partly in the gateway passage. This entrance may have been protected from the landward

side by a curtain wall bulging out from the main wall on either side, but little of it remains. Towards the southern side of the headland, both wall and ditch peter out for nature to take over the defensive work with rocky outcrops and steep slopes.

No permanent dwelling sites were found within the fort, which legend says was the work of a local giant, but the remains of stone-edged fields can be seen clearly on the coastal slope overlooking the site. These are almost certainly as old as the castle. A large part of these cliffs, including the fields and the castle, were given to the National Trust in 1935-6 by a group of people calling themselves 'Ferguson's Gang'.

Above & below: *Maen Castle (67).*

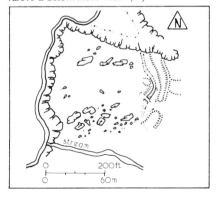

68 Mulfra Vean Courtyard House Village, New Mill.

NG 453349. *Marked as:* **settlement**.
Beside footpath from Mulfra Quoit (Site 7) to Mulfra Farm which is reached by lane running NW from New Mill.

There are at least three courtyard houses in this settlement, the clearest of which is in a field on the western side of the path. This house, excavated by the West Cornwall Field Club in 1954, has walls up to 3ft (0.9m) high with stonework visible in places. The courtyard, entered from the east side, has a long room on its north side and two smaller chambers on the

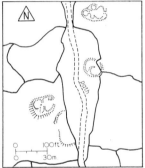

south. The entrance to the round living room is indicated by a very large, upright jambstone.

Just to the south of this house is a terraced area with some walling along its edge. This may have been the site of a courtyard house.

Another house, intersected by the hedge, is on the opposite side of the footpath. Stones built into the hedge indicate that the entrance to this house faced north-east, but the building is badly mutilated and only hints of its original plan can now be seen.

A further courtyard house lies close by to the north and, although battered, its plan can be seen clearly. The courtyard, entered from the east, has two small chambers on either side and the round room still has its doorjambs standing. The houses of this village were built on artificial terraces.

69 Pendeen Vau, Fogou, Pendeen.

NG 384355. *Marked as:* **fogou**.
Permission to visit this site must be sought from Pendeen Manor Farm, off N side of lane leading from B3306 at Pendeen to Pendeen Watch lighthouse.

Pendeen Vau (*vau* is a shortened form of the word *fogo*) lies just behind the beautiful sixteenth-century Pendeen Manor, birthplace of Dr William Borlase, the eighteenth-century 'father of Cornish archaeology'.

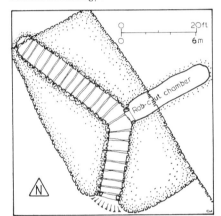

The fogou is a superb structure, its entrance passage being within the thickness of an ancient and immense Cornish hedge, which is 8ft (2.4m) high, 15ft (4.6m) thick and 49ft (15m) long.

From the entrance, the main passage descends steeply, then levels out and turns sharply to the left where it becomes a long, straight passage ending with a tiny hole in the roof near the foot of the hedge above it. The total length of this passage is 56½ft (17.2m).

At the angle of the passage is a small, well-built portal 2ft (0.6m) wide and just 1½ft (0.5m) high, leading into a closed chamber which is cut from the solid clay with no supporting stonework at all. Semi-circular in section, it is 24ft (7.3m) long, 5ft (1.5m) wide and 4ft (1.2m) high.

A feature of this fogou is the collection of large, loose stones which cover much of the floor and which have not fallen from either the corbelled walls or the heavily lintelled roof.

Pendeen Vau was at one time believed to be of vast extent, reaching the sea or even the Isles of Scilly! Another legend is of the Spirit of the Vau, a woman in white who appears at the mouth of the fogou on Christmas mornings. She carries a red rose in her mouth and any who see her will die within the year – so don't visit Pendeen Vau on Christmas morning!

70 Porthmeor Courtyard House Village, Treen (North).

NG 434371. *Not marked.*
Ask for directions at Porthmeor Farm, on B3306 just W of the Gurnard's Head Hotel at Treen.

The first of the courtyard house villages to be excavated, Porthmeor probably began as an open hut circle settlement, then, during the second century AD, two or three courtyard houses were built within an oval fortification which also enclosed four terraces and a number of hut circles.

The fortification, a thick stone wall up to 8ft (2.4m) high, measures 280ft (85m) by 230ft (70m) and has two entrances. The main entrance, on the south side, led into a paved court, on the east side of which is the entrance to a courtyard house (House 2). This has a round room with a back door, two small oval chambers on the south side of the courtyard and a long room on the north side. Also on the north side of the house is a small hut which was probably entered from the exterior. Walls survive to a height of 3½ft (1.1m). Three other huts open onto the entrance court and a fourth lies against the inside of the defensive wall to the north.

The south-western entrance to the fortified area also led into a paved court, on the east side of which is a possible, but unexcavated, courtyard house and a hut circle in which was found a tin-smelting furnace.

On the opposite side of the entrance court, built against the enclosing wall, are a hut circle and another courtyard house (House 1). Like House 2, this has a round room with back door, two small chambers on one side of the courtyard and a long room on the other. On the east side of this house is a length of paved road leading to a circular area, also paved.

Two Roman coins were found in the round room of House 1, dated to the reign of Marcus Aurelius and minted in AD 174-5. These probably indicate some measure of contact with Roman traders, most likely in tin.

Just south-west of the fortified area are the fragmentary remains of a further courtyard house, around the round room of which runs a roofless but fine above-ground fogou. This consists of a curving passage 43ft (13m) long, the inner 24ft (7.3m) of which were roofed by the corbelling technique. The outer part of the passage was roofed by lintels. The passage is 5ft (1.5m) wide, with walling remaining to a height of 5½ft (1.7m). Excavation revealed a drainage system under the floor, but failed to ascertain whether the fogou ever led into a hut circle attached to the north side of the courtyard house.

The occupation of Porthmeor continued at least until AD 400 and possibly even as late as the sixth century. Excavations were carried out by the then newly-formed West Cornwall Field Club in 1933-9, under the direction of the late Lt. Col. F.C. Hirst, the pioneer of courtyard house study. The village is still referred to locally as 'Colonel Hirst's' village.

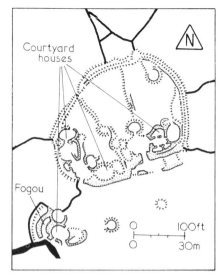

Above & below: *Porthmeor site (70)*

71 Sperris and Wicca Hut Circle Settlements, Zennor.

NG 473384 and 473386. *Marked as:* **settlement**.
Footpath leads straight uphill from S side of B3306 1¼ miles E of Zennor at NG 472388. Wicca Round lies on W side of path just before last field wall. Sperris Croft is on the very top of the ridge.

Sperris Croft consists of seven hut circles strung out in a line along the ridge more than 700ft (214m) above sea level, exposed and windswept. The huts measure between 20 and 46ft (6.1m and 14m) in diameter and were excavated by the West Cornwall Field Club in 1956-7. The second and fourth huts from the east have a small chamber attached to their southern sides. Although very clearly seen, little more than foundations remain as stone from them was used in the building of two nearby mines, Wheal Sandwich and Wheal Sperris. It is ironic that very little now remains of either of these mines.

Wicca Round was also excavated by the West Cornwall Field Club, in 1956-7. Lying within a fairly extensive field system, it consists of a

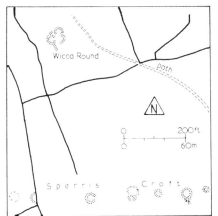

Above & below: *Sperris and Wicca sites (71)*

compact though mutilated group of three huts arranged in a tight triangular plan. There is more undergrowth here than on the top of the ridge, which makes Wicca Round more difficult to observe than Sperris Croft.

Both settlements date from at least the early Iron Age.

72 Trencrom Castle Hill Fort, Lelant. NT.

NG 518362. *Marked as:* **fort**.
Road from A3074, near its junction with A30, to Cripple's Ease passes S side of hill where there is a small car park with steep footpath leading to summit.

Iron Age chieftains certainly appreciated the superb strategic position of Trencrom Hill with its views over the trading ports of the Hayle estuary and St. Michael's Mount and the entire isthmus between. They turned its craggy summit into a fort by building a great wall around it. For much of its course, the construction technique resembles that of Maen Castle *(Site 67)*: two rows of great upright blocks with an infill of rubble. It may, therefore, be of the same age – the fourth century BC. The builders were aided by the numerous rugged outcrops on the hill and the wall wanders from one to the next, incorporating each into the defences. As a result, the plan of the fort is irregular, roughly pear-shaped and measuring 450ft (137m) from north to south, by 300ft (91m).

The internal height of the wall varies from 2ft (0.6m) to 7½ft (2.2m), its outer face being much higher due to the sudden steepness of the hillsides which also removed any necessity for an outer ditch. The thickness of the wall is sometimes as much as 15ft (4.6m).

It is not known whether an entrance ever existed at the northern end of the fort, between two large rock-piles, but two fine gateways survive, opposite each other on the east and west sides. Both have upright jambstones, slightly inturned rampart-ends, and sunken tracks leading downhill from them.

A large number of hut circles lie within the defended area; as many as 16 have been counted, but only about four can be seen clearly (not to be confused with a number of recent pits in the south-east corner of the fort).

There are two wells on the hill. One, known as the 'Giant's Well', is well-hidden on the eastern slope of the hill and the other, enlarged in

recent times, is at the foot of the westernmost of the twin crags at the north end of the fort. Traces of a hidden path leading from the inside of the fort can be seen, along with an overflow channel and remains of a small protective wall.

Trencrom Castle has never been excavated, but pottery thrown up by moles and rabbits has dated it to at least 200 BC and, as mentioned above, the building technique may indicate an even earlier date. Traces of occupation as late as the eighth century AD have also been found.

Legend connects the hill fort with giants who are said to have built it; especially the giant Trecrobm (a variant form of the name Trencrom) who is always associated with his titanic colleague Cormoran of St. Michael's Mount. This ancient belief in the Trencrom giants becomes easier to understand when considering the sheer size of some of the blocks used in the construction of the wall. The giants are gone, but their treasure, says legend, remains buried deep inside the hill. Woe betide the treasure seeker, for it is jealously guarded by hordes of spriggans, ugly and vicious hobgoblins reputed to be the ghosts of the giants.

Trencrom Hill and its fort were given to the National Trust in 1946 as a memorial to those Cornish men and women who gave their lives during the two World Wars, surely one of the finest war memorials anywhere in Britain.

Trencrom Castle (72).

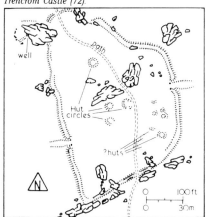

73 Treryn Dinas Cliff Castle, Treen (South). NT.

NG 397221. *Marked as:* **Treryn Dinas**.
Path. To Logan Rock and Treen Cliff, leaves the village of Treen, just off B3315. There is a small car park in the village. Alternatively, cliff path between Porthcurno and Penberth Cove passes the site.

As the National Trust property of Trencrom Hill *(Site 72)* is the most spectacularly sited hill fort in West Penwith, so this site, also National Trust land, is the most spectacular of the cliff castles.

To reach the famous Logan (pronounced Loggan) Rock, which stands out on the tip of the headland, no fewer than four lines of defence are passed through.

The outermost is an immense earth embankment 300yds (274m) long and up to 21ft (6.4m) high, fronted by a ditch which reaches a depth of 6½ft (2.0m). This massive rampart spans the base of the headland in a great arc from Polpry Cove on the west to Haldinas Cove on the east.

200ft (61m) to the south is a central complex of defences. On the flat top of the headland, this consists of two ramparts and ditches. The outermost of these ditches has, for part of its course, a faint counterscarp bank along its outer edge which some have mistakenly interpreted as another rampart. This ditch spans the

headland from the cliff above Polpry Cove, close to the terminal of the outer rampart, to the foot of a vertical rockface on the eastern side. The bank within it, up to 6½ft (2.0m) high, also starts below this rockface and describes a pronounced arc to follow the brink of the steep western coastal slope. Here, an offshooting bank 4ft (1.2m) high follows the ditch to the cliff edge.

A shallow ditch then follows the foot of a slight ridge on which was built the second of these central ramparts. Beginning, on the eastern side, at the top of the rockface, it then follows the line of the ridge and joins onto the previous rampart. This bank, now less than 4ft (1.2m) high, was originally faced with stone but it has been extensively robbed.

The fourth line of defence crosses the headland's extremely narrow neck, below a steep, boulder-strewn slope. Here a 9ft (2.7m) deep ditch, with signs of a counterscarp bank, fronts a strong stone wall 6ft (1.8m) high and 10ft (3.0m) thick. The ditch is crossed by a central causeway to the gateway which still has both jambstones standing. Behind each end of the wall are the remains of a hut circle, although half of the western one has been eroded away.

The remainder of the headland is naturally fortified by huge vertical crags resembling ruined

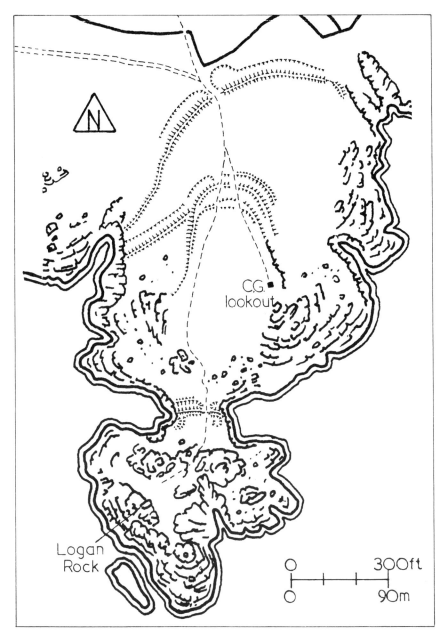

Logan
Rock

300ft

90m

turrets, and battlements and a narrow pass between them is the only access to the interior.

Although this cliff castle is unexcavated, it is believed that the four lines of defence were built at various times between the third and first centuries BC.

The legends of Treryn Dinas could fill a volume; tales of giants, witches and the beautiful Small People; of the headland's magical origin and of Merlin Ambrosius. One writer said of this cliff castle that, 'it is a pity that no Arthurian connections can be found for it', yet one legend clearly states that 'Treryn Castle was in the possession of Arthur for some time'. Also, this is one of the many places where Merlin is said to lie imprisoned forever by magic, supposedly in a cave beneath the Logan Rock.

A book about archaeology is not really the place to talk about this naturally-balanced 70-ton boulder, but two common fallacies must be laid. First, when Lt. Goldsmith and the crew of the *Nimble* levered the rock off its perch in 1824, it did not fall into the sea, nor off the rockpile onto the turf below. It caught in the crevice on its eastern side, else recovery would have been impossible. The second fallacy is that the stone no longer rocks. It does; although it takes some effort. The secret is to give a series of strong pushes to the south-western corner of the stone.

The tackle used by Lt. Goldsmith and Captain Giddy to replace the Logan Rock was afterwards used to re-erect the fallen neolithic Penwith tomb of Lanyon Quoit *(Site 6)*.

Left: *Plan of Treryn Dinas site (73). The fort itself is pictured opposite.*

74 Trevean Round, Morvah.

NG 413353. *Not marked.*
In corner of a field adjoining E side of Penzance – Morvah road, and just above a modern bungalow, after taking right fork ½ mile NE of Bosullow Common.

This is a fine, but little-known round some 125ft (38m) in diameter, surrounded by a wall up to 6ft (1.8m) high and, on the eastern side, as much as 25ft (7.6m) thick. The entrance faces west and it is not known whether it ever contained huts; no excavations have been carried out here.

To the north, on the edge of moorland at the western foot of Watch Croft, are the remains of a courtyard house village where three houses can be seen. The first, at NG 413357, has a west-facing entrance, now blocked, and its low remains show only a long room and round room leading off the courtyard. The other two houses, at NG 413358, are built on terraces. That on the upper terrace is difficult to make out, but it appears to consist of a courtyard with three rooms leading off; the round room, a small, oval chamber on the north side and a long room on

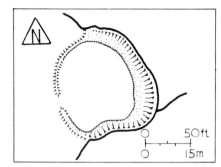

Above & below: *Trevean Round (74)*

the south, with the entrance to the house beside it. Behind the house are the remains of a hut, reached by a back door from the round room. On the terrace below it is the third courtyard house which seems to have been adapted in post-mediaeval times, but the shapes of the courtyard and round room can still be seen, as can a satellite hut attached to the south side of the round room. A nearby above-ground fogou was destroyed in 1913.

Many of the present fields here, on both sides of the road, can plainly be seen to have been built on prehistoric terraces.

75 Trewern Round, Newbridge.

NG 433320. *Marked as:* **Trewern Round.**
300yds (274m) SE of Trewern Farm, on E side of lane from A30 at Newbridge to Penzance – Morvah road.

This small, oval enclosure, 180ft (55m) by 150ft (46m), stands on a spur between two valleys. It once contained hut circles, but they vanished long ago and four or five huts just outside it were destroyed sometime before 1848.

The round is defined by a single, unditched stone wall, but it is not certain how much of it is original. The north-eastern half certainly is, but the other half, punctured by two modern gateways, one blocked up, seems to be more recent, with a wall 6½ft (2.0m) high. The north-eastern wall reaches a height of 7ft (2.1m) and the interior on that side is raised 5ft (1.5m) above the level of the adjoining field.

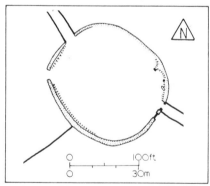

The round has two entrances; at the north-west and south-east. The latter has both gate-jambs in place, one a tall, slim stone 7ft (2.1m) high, the other a great square block 4ft (1.2m) high, supported on smaller stones. A length of trackway leads from each entrance. On the east side of the enclosure is an erect stone 4ft (1.2m) high, built against the inside of the wall.

100yds (91m) to the north-west of the round is a Bronze Age menhir, 6ft (1.8m) tall. Another, which stood in a nearby field, was destroyed in 1958.

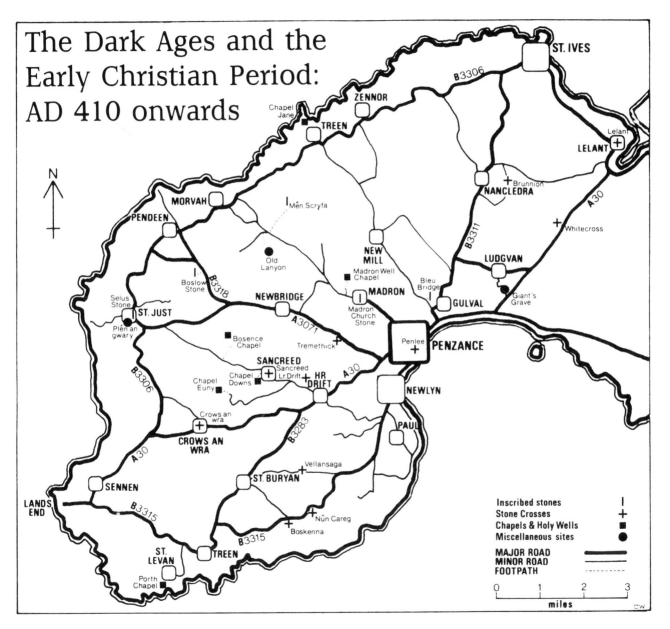

The Dark Ages and the
Early Christian Period:
AD 410 onwards

Inscribed stones
Stone Crosses
Chapels & Holy Wells
Miscellaneous sites

MAJOR ROAD
MINOR ROAD
FOOTPATH

0   1   2   3
miles

In AD 410, the Roman emperor Honorius informed the native people of Britain that they must look to their own defence. Rome had growing troubles of her own and her forces were moving out, never to return. So, after nearly 400 years, the Roman occupation of Britain came to an end, leaving the island open to the attacks of the Teutonic races from across the North Sea. By AD 450, the Angles, Saxons, Jutes and Danes had begun their invasion, catching the Britons virtually defenceless. After four centuries of comparative peace, the arts of war were almost forgotten and leaders were scarce.

During the following five hundred years, the invaders pressed slowly westward, the only period of respite coming in the early sixth century. Towards the end of the fifth century, the Britons had at last found a leader, Aurelius Ambrosius. Reviving the old Roman cavalry techniques, this man rose to lead a stubborn resistance force against the invaders. His success was largely due to the fact that the Anglo-Saxons had yet to master the art of horsemanship, and the people of Britain had been riding horses since the Bronze Age. Ambrosius did not live to see the finest victory, which occurred between the years AD 500 and 520. This fell to his successor, a brilliant general named Arthur. The Battle of Mount Badon, probably in Wiltshire, halted a major Saxon advance into the west country, and the victory was so complete as to ensure nearly fifty years of peace. Some disheartened Saxons even left Britain and went back to their homeland.

The only piece of historical evidence to link Arthur and Cornwall is in the *Annales Cambriae*, which was compiled in the tenth century from older material. Against the year AD 537 (or 539) it lists: 'the Battle of Camlan in which Arthur and Medraut were slain and there was grief in Ireland and Cornwall'. As Cornwall is a possible location for this unknown battlefield, this could imply that Arthur, a general not a king, fought the battle in Cornwall against Medraut (Mordred), whose army of rebels included Irish mercenaries. We know that there was an incursion of Irishmen into north-eastern Cornwall during the late fifth and early sixth centuries.

Welsh triads and tales from *The Mabinogion*, all extremely old, tell that Arthur's home (as opposed to his headquarters) was at Kelliwic on the north coast of Cornwall, possibly the Iron Age fort of Castle Killibury near Wadebridge. A very old legend connects Arthur with West Penwith, and it is odd that a number of recent books about him, some locally published, have left out this story.

It tells of a battle fought by Arthur and nine local chieftains against a party from a marauding Danish fleet which had landed at Gwynver, just north of Sennen Cove. The battle, won decisively by the Britons, took place at Vellan-druchar and there are two places so named: one, a mile east of St. Buryan; the other near Tremethick Cross, two miles west of Penzance. Should the legend be true, the latter would be the more likely place as it was on the path of an ancient trackway from Land's End and quite close to the hill fort of Lesingey Round *(Site 65)*. The legend also describes the alarm system which brought Arthur westwards: a chain of bonfires on the Cornish beacon hills. After making certain that the Danish ships were of no further use to any chance survivors, the victors held a feast on the sacred rock called the Table Mên, which can still be seen within the entrance to Mayon Farm about ¼ mile north of Sennen church. According to the legend, Merlin was there, and uttered one of his cheerful prophecies:

> The Northmen wild once more shall land
> And leave their bones on Escalls' sand.
> The soil of Vellan-druchar's plain
> Again shall take a sanguine stain;
> And o'er the millwheel roll a flood
> Of Danish mixed with Cornish blood.
> When thus the vanquished find no tomb
> Expect the dreadful day of doom.

Irish and Welsh arrivals in Cornwall were not great in number and many were probably here only on a temporary basis. The most interesting of them were the famous 'saints' of Cornwall.

The Celtic races of Britain were becoming Christian as early as the fourth century, and these saints were missionaries of both sexes. Most came from Ireland and Wales, notably Saints Piran, Petroc, Ia, Erc, Brychan and his numerous saintly children – probably not his offspring, but junior priests under his leadership. Other saints came from Brittany and a few were Cornish. Among the latter are Selyf and Justin, the sons of Cornwall's King Gerent, who became known as St. (Se)levan and St. Just. Their father's name also became saintly, and is commemorated in the name of Gerrans, a village on the Roseland peninsula. It was W.C. Borlase who dubbed the late fifth and sixth centuries as the 'Age of the Saints'.

After the 'Age of the Saints', Christianity became widespread and little, independant monasteries sprang up. Among these were Dinurrin (Bodmin), Landocco (St. Kew), Lamanna near Looe, St.

Germans and, one of the oldest of all, that founded by St. Juliot on the Island at Tintagel, which dates from the late fifth century. In the ninth century, the Cornish bishop Kenstec of Dinurrin was said to profess obedience to Ceolnoth, Archbishop of Canterbury and, at the beginning of the following century, King Edward created the see of Crediton, instructing his bishop Eadwulf to stamp out the Cornish resistance to papal decrees.

Under Athelstan, St. Germans became the primary Cornish monastery owing allegiance to the Celtic bishop Conan. Another small religious centre at the shrine of St. Beriana, now St. Buryan in West Penwith, was granted a royal charter by the same king, possibly at the same time as his treaty with the Cornish king Howal in AD 927. The early Cornish diocese came to an end in 1026, when it was included in the see of Crediton. Forty years later the Normans, descendants of the Vikings, landed and before long the true conquest of Cornwall by the Norman barons was complete. The Duchy was created in 1337.

Throughout the Iron Age and the Dark Ages, Cornwall had a number of kings, mostly little more than tribal chieftains, under the dominion of the King of Dumnonia, which comprised Cornwall, Devon and part of Somerset. Fragmentary remains exist of the king lists of Dumnonia. These include Gerent, Constantine and Cynvawr, or Cunomorus, whose name appears on a sixth-century inscribed stone near Fowey (Drustans – Tristan? – lies here, son of Cunomorus). Breton sources give his name more fully: Marcus Cunomorus, or King Mark. With this stone, legend comes to life.

Some of the inscribed stones, which originated in the fifth century, hint at the names of smaller chieftains: Rialobran and Cunoval for example, of the Mên Scryfa *(Site 90)*, must have been of local royalty, because of the meaning of their names, and the Celts did not give their names as lightly as we do today. These inscribed stones commemorate the first Cornishmen whose names we know.

Doniert, or Dunjarth, who was drowned in the River Fowey in AD 878, is often said to have been the last of the Cornish kings, but at least two more reigned in the far west of Cornwall. The Penlee House Cross *(Site 93)*, dated to between AD 900 and 925, bears the name of a King Ricatus, and finally there was his probable successor King Howal, who signed the treaty of peace and allegiance to King Athelstan in AD 927. Howal was probably the last of the Cornish kings.

For most of the native Cornish, Dark Age life was more or less as it had been throughout the Iron Age although, by the time of the Roman departure, they were beginning to abandon their hut circle and courtyard house villages to set up farming communities, or 'trevs', on lower, more fertile ground, often around the cells of the new missionaries. Many of these were to become the present day villages and towns. Nevertheless, word was filtering down from up-country of the Teutonic invasion and, as the years went by, of their westward advance.

By as early as the end of the fifth century, many of the Cornish were migrating across the Channel to settle with their cousins in Brittany, and those who stayed prepared for a dogged resistance. During the sixth century, Iron Age forts throughout the south-west were re-occupied and sometimes modified. In West Penwith, the most notable example of this was Chûn Castle *(Site 54)*, where the entrance was craftily altered. The foundations still visible in the interior of the fort are also of sixth century origin.

The Saxon victory at Dyrham, near Bath, in AD 577, cut all land connections between the Celts of Wales and Cornwall and, as a result, their common British language began to develop into two distinct languages. Today, Cornish, or Kernewek to give it its proper name, is far closer to Breton than to the possibly Gaelic-influenced Welsh. It is seen, albeit in a corrupted form, in the vast majority of Cornish place-names. It ceased to be a mother-tongue in the eighteenth century, but never died out completely, and today there is renewed interest in the language.

Not until the eighth century did the Saxons, now civilised Christians, reach the River Tamar to find a resiliant race who did not savour the idea of being conquered. The first recorded battle was at Hehil, probably Slaughter Bridge near Camelford, in AD 722. A Cornish victory ensured an uneasy peace until AD 825 when they again won the day at Galford, on the Devon side of the Tamar. Unfortunately, the names of the battle-leaders have not survived.

The turning point came in AD 838. King Egbert's massed Saxon army threatened and the Cornish went to confront them at Hingston Down near Callington, aided by the unlikeliest of allies. A fleet of Danish Vikings had appeared on Cornwall's south coast and, as they had little love for the Saxons, joined with the Cornish forces against Egbert. But the Cornu-Danish army was soundly defeated, opening the flood gates for Saxon settlement which, however, was mostly confined to the easternmost parts. As can be seen from place-names, Devon became almost totally Saxon and was incorporated into the kingdom of Wessex, but Cornwall remained Celtic even though, after the coming of King Athelstan in AD 927, she fell under the rule of Saxon kings.

Even then Cornwall retained some measure of independence, for it was Athelstan himself who fixed the River Tamar as the boundary between the Saxon kingdom of Wessex and the 'West Welsh' or Cornish. To this day, no legal changes have been made to this declaration, except to make Cornwall a duchy, and, on paper, Cornwall remains an entity apart; a semi-independent Celtic state with allegiance to the throne of Britain. Cornwall cannot be said to have been truly conquered by the Saxons; subjugated, perhaps, but not truly conquered. That is, until the coming of the Normans.

It was during the ninth century that Cornwall gained its present name. The Celtic inhabitants had always called their land Cerneu, or Kernow, latinised by the Romans to Cornubia. The Saxons took this name and joined it to their own word Wealas, which meant strangers or foreigners and from which comes the name Wales. Over the years, Cerneu-wealas was corrupted and abbreviated to Cornwall.

Various monuments remain from the Dark Age and early Christian period. The inscribed stones are Christian memorial stones, inscribed in bad Latin and mostly containing Latinised forms of Cornish names. Irish names occur now and again, and half a dozen examples in mid and east Cornwall are additionally carved with the curious Irish Ogam script. The majority of inscribed stones in West Penwith date from between the fifth and seventh centuries.

Dotted around the Land's End peninsula are tiny, ancient chapels, frequently associated with holy wells, springs which are often attributed with legendary healing and oracular powers. The chapels may date from as early as the eighth century, some are rather later, but a few may even have originated with their associated 'saint'.

The stone crosses for which Cornwall is famous originated in the ninth century, and most were set up along the traditional paths to church. Some of the larger and more ornate examples stand in churchyards, but a number of crosses have been moved from their original positions. Only a selection of the best examples are included in this book, for there are a large number of them in West Penwith alone.

Also included here are three miscellaneous sites, two dating from the mediaeval period and one from the Civil War. This last is included because there is a faint possibility of a Dark Age origin.

76 Bleu Bridge Inscribed Stone, Gulval.

NG 477318. *Not marked.*
Beside footpath leading downhill off E side of Penzance – Zennor road 200yds (180m) NW of its junction with B3311.

Standing near the footbridge in Barlowena Bottoms is a stone 5½ft (1.7m) high, fairly clearly inscribed with the words: QVENATAVCI IC DINVI FILIVS – Quenataucus (lies) here, the son of Dinuus.

The fact that these names are Irish illustrates that the isthmus of Penwith was still a centre of commerce and travel during the Dark Age. The inscription, in bad Latin, dates from the sixth century and is not accompanied by an Irish Ogam inscription.

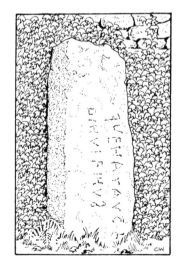

77 Bosence Chapel, Sancreed.

NG 407305. *Not marked.*
On N side of a field just W of Bosence Farm, reached by lane N from St. Just – Sancreed road.

This mediaeval chapel owes its continued existence to having being utilised in the field hedge. Measuring 23ft (7.0m) by 12ft (3.7m) internally, its walls are 2ft (0.6m) thick and are now from 3ft (0.9m) to 7ft (2.1m) high. The foundations were cut into the hillside and the entrance, near the western end of the south wall, was 3ft (0.9m) in width, before being blocked up in recent times.

In a hedge near Botrea Farm, ¼ mile to the west, are the heads of two cusped windows which came from the chapel; presumably from

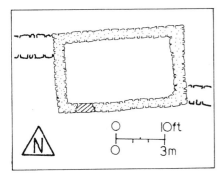

Bosence Chapel (77)

the west end. Some other carved stones can be seen on site. These window heads have been dated to the fifteenth century, but may well have been later additions. The chapel itself is probably a good deal earlier than that. Only excavation, which has not yet taken place, can provide a likely date.

A tale is told by William Bottrell of a certain Uter Bosence, who found himself here in thick mist, and at the dead of night, after attending midsummer eve festivities on the top of Trannack Hill. To his horror, he saw that the ruined chapel was occupied by hideous creatures; man-like, but with the heads of adders! They were led by a being in the form of a great black goat, which stood erect on its hind legs, and which tried to involve Uter in a grotesque dance. The terrified man struck the creature with his blackthorn stick and fled, only just escaping with his life. Needless to add, poor Uter took a long time to recover from his ordeal. Were these creatures 'sprights and spriggans' as the legend tells, or did Uter stumble on a Black Magic ceremony with the participants in hideous costume? These ceremonies were, and, for that matter, still are, often held in ruined or desecrated chapels and churches.

Below left: *Bosence Chapel (77)*. Below right: *Boskenna Stone Cross (78)*.

78 Boskenna Stone Cross, St. Buryan.

NG 425243. *Marked as:* **crosses**.
Beside B3315 at junction with road to St. Buryan.

This very old circular cross-head is curiously mounted on a stone roller, millstone and stone cider press. The front of the cross-head bears a Christ figure, carved in relief; the rear shows a wheel-cross formed by four triangular incisions.

Just to the west, on the south side of the B3315 at NG 420241, near the drive entrance to Boskenna House, is the Boskenna Gate cross, a round-headed monument with a Latin cross carved in relief on both sides with the lower limb of each running down the length of the shaft. The head was evidently broken off at some time, but has been successfully repositioned.

79 The Boslow Stone, Inscribed Stone, Pendeen.

NG 393331. *Not marked.*
In overgrown junction of lanes leading from B3318 to Carnyorth Farm.

This 5ft (1.5m) high stone was formerly known as 'Crowze East' (*Crows Ust* – St. Just cross) and stands on the boundary of St. Just and Sancreed parishes.

Its southern face bears a simple incised cross; the western side has a much-worn inscription, probably of the sixth or seventh century. The words *JAC-T VENA* can just be made out, probably the remains of an inscription reading *HIC JACIT VENA* (Here lies Vena).

80 Brunnion Carn Stone Cross, Nancledra.

NG 504360. *Marked as:* **cross**.
By side of lane S from Cripple's Ease to Ludgvan.

This fine, tall cross is set on a large square base. Both front and back have a Latin cross cut in relief with the lower limb extending down the length of the shaft.

At one time, it stood dramatically in the centre of a small pool of water.

Brunnion Carn Cross (80)

81 Chapel Downs, Chapel and Holy Well, Sancreed.

NG 418293. *Not marked.*
Beside footpath leading SW from Bird-in-Hand (formerly Glebe) Farm, opposite Sancreed church.

A modern cross, erected in 1910, stands close to the remains of this tiny chapel which measures just 14ft (4.3m) by 6½ft (2.0m) internally. The walls, 2½ft (0.7m) thick, now stand from only 2ft (0.6m) to 4ft (1.2m) high. The entrance, at the south-western corner, has a carved stone lying in it. It is a small, simple round-headed arch, probably from the doorway. Sherds of pottery found outside the south wall of the chapel were dated to the fiteenth or sixteenth centuries, but the chapel itself is likely to be a good deal older than that.

Close by is the holy well, probably dedicated to St. Sancred, although this is by no means certain. It is an underground structure, approached by a flight of stone steps. The well is a iong, narrow chamber with a corbelled roof and a lintel over the entrance. It was once thought to extend beneath the chapel but, in fact, it stops short of it. A stone-lined overflow channel leads from the well entrance towards the east and the remains of a bridge over it can be seen near the top of the well steps.

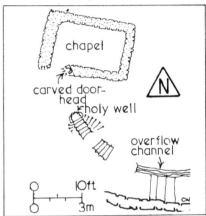

Chapel Downs (81)

82 Chapel Euny Holy Well, Sancreed.

NG 400289. Marked as: **well.**
Beside footpath leading W from Carn Euny Iron Age courtyard house village (Site 50).

The holy well of St. Uny, lying beside an ancient track and reached by descending seven stone steps to the beautifully clear spring, is enclosed in a covered recess. A number of large stones are placed around the top of the well opening, two of them are worked and once formed parts of an arch from either a doorway or a window. These probably came from the tiny chapel which once stood nearby but has now been lost, destroyed some centuries ago.

The water of Chapel Euny well was reputed to have the virtue of healing most children's diseases, although its capabilities were restricted to the first three Wednesdays in May.

A little known-fact is that there are two wells at Chapel Euny. The second stands just a few paces west of its better-known neighbour and is enclosed in the remains of four walls.

83 Chapel Jane, Treen (North).

NG 434383. Marked as: **chapel.**
On cliffedge at eastern base of Gurnard's Head, beside footpath to Treen Cove.

Built near a now lost holy well, the original chapel was 16ft (4.9m) long by 8ft (2.4m) wide, but at some later date was extended 6ft (1.8m) westwards at a width of 9ft (2.7m). The walls are 2ft (0.6m) thick and survive to about 2½ft (0.8m) high. The chapel has a stone bench along the north wall, an altar recess at the east end and a drain through the south wall. A large slab lying nearby was the mensa or altar slab. The original doorway was in the south wall but was at some time blocked up, another being built through the west wall. Excavated by Vivien Russell and Peter Pool in 1964-6, the chapel was shown to be at least of the twelfth century and may well be even older. Erosion has now brought the cliffedge to within inches of the north-east corner. Although the chapel was built in a natural hollow, the remains of an earthwork just to the north may be part of an enclosure, or 'lan', around the building. The site of the holy well was probably just to the south of the chapel,

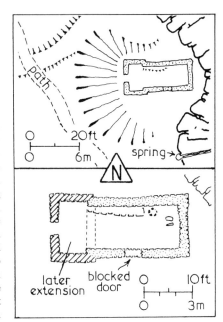

where a spring rises on the cliff-edge.

The name of the chapel does not derive from a female patron saint, but from the Cornish word *yeyn*, bleak, cold.

84 Crows-an-wra Stone Cross, Crows-an-wra.

NG 395276. *Marked as:* **crosses**.
Beside A30, at junction of road from Crows-an-wra to B3306 (Land's End Aerodrome).

Standing beside a curious and ornate milestone, this fine cross has given its name to the hamlet surrounding it. A wheel-headed cross is carved on both sides, with the lower limb running down the shaft which is set into a stepped granite plinth.

Crows-an-wra (*Crows an wragh* – the witch's cross) may have been named after Harry the Hermit, a former incumbent of the chapel that once stood on the great barrow topping the hill of Chapel Carn Brea *(Site 4)*, which rises above the hamlet.

Disliked by the Dean of St. Buryan and others, Harry, who could speak both Cornish and English, was accused of being a sorceror. His sins were said to be in spoiling the crops of those who crossed him; sitting on the brink of the huge cliff at Tol-Pedn without fear; and fashioning a ship from a sheep's shoulder blade and sailing it from the Funnel Cave at Tol-Pedn (Tol-Pedn-Penwith, now, for some obscure reason, called Gwennap Head).

History does not recall the fate of Harry the Hermit, but it seems that his memory lives on in the name of the hamlet and its ancient cross.

85 Giant's Grave, Linear Earthwork, Ludgvan.

NG 507322. *Not marked.*
Lane from A30, 1/4 mile NE of its junction with A394, to Ludgvan – Gulval road passes through the site.

This linear defensive earthwork has 450yds (410m) of its length remaining and reaches a height of 11ft (3.3m). A former ditch on its south-eastern side has virtually disappeared, and it is not known what its original length was. It is generally agreed that it was raised in the Civil War, prior to the siege of St. Michael's Mount, but its position poses the question of whether or not an already existing bank was

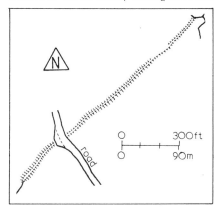

Left: *The Crows-an-Wra stone cross (84), standing next to a 'modern' milestone.*

strengthened for use in the Civil War. The Giant's Grave closely resembles the Bolster Bank, near St. Agnes, and the Giant's Hedge between the Fowey and Looe rivers, which were territorial boundaries set up during the Dark Age. It may be that the Giant's Grave also had its origins at this time, perhaps cutting off the entire Penwith peninsula. Excavation alone will reveal the truth and this has yet to take place.

86 Lelant Stone Crosses, Lelant.

NG 548378. *Marked as:* **crosses.**
In Lelant churchyard.

Two crosses stand within the churchyard. One is of the wheel-headed type on a heavy shaft which bulges somewhat in the centre. Both sides of the small head have four triangular recesses forming the shape of a cross and surrounding a central boss.

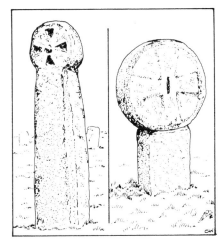

The Lelant crosses.

The other cross, on the south side of the church, has a large round head set on a squat modern shaft. One side of the cross-head, scarred by drill marks, has a figure with truncated legs, which probably extended onto the original shaft. The rear of the cross-head, which came from Trevethoe, a mile or so away, has a cross cut in low relief.

Two more crosses can be seen in the adjoining cemetery. One, on a square base, has its cross in relief. The other also has a large Christ figure which extends down much of the shaft, this shown by a deeply incised outline. A surrounding bead also continues down the shaft.

87 Lower Drift Stone Cross, Drift.

NG 437288. *Not marked.*
In woodland below Drift-Sancreed road just SE of Drift Dam.

This unusual cross is a large, wedge-shaped hunk of granite with a Latin cross cut in relief on front and back.

At one time, it lay on its side further up the slope but, while attempts were being made to re-erect it, it rolled down the hillside to where it now stands.

88 Madron Chapel and Holy Well, Madron

NG 447328. *Marked as:* **chapel.**
Reached by a lane, signposted 'Wishing Well', and footpath, leading off N side of Penzance – Morvah road, ¼ mile W of Madron.

The holy well of St. Madern, supposedly of curative and prophetic powers, is a natural, stone lined spring. It can be seen that old beliefs die hard in West Penwith; the bushes around the well are still hung with votive strips of rag.

The well chapel is about 100yds (91m) to the north-east, overhung by trees, and has been restored following the damage inflicted on it by Shrubsall's Roundheads. It has been dated to around the twelfth century, but the lower courses are probably pre-Norman.

Often wrongly referred to as a baptistery, the chapel is a tiny, roofless building with walls 2½ft (0.8m) thick and 6ft (1.8m) high. Its internal dimensions are 21ft (6.4m) by 11ft (3.3m) and the doorway is, unusually, in the north wall. Still remaining inside the building are stone side benches, a rough chancel step and an altar slab with a square recess to receive a portable altar.

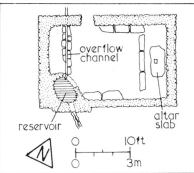

A tiny rivulet enters the building through the south wall and collects in a small, rectangular, corbelled reservoir before flowing out in overflow across the floor of the chapel in a stone-lined channel, and out through the north wall. This curious reservoir has often been mistaken for the holy well.

89 Madron Church Inscribed Stone, Madron.

NG 453318. *Not marked.*
In W end of Madron church.

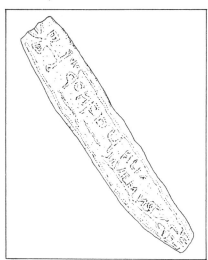

This fascinating stone was discovered in 1936, built into the south-west wall of the church and concealed under layers of plaster. It was subsequently removed and set up in its present position.

At the top of the 6ft (1.8m) high stone is a strange cross with leaf-like arms, resting on a bar with looped ends, probably a late and ornate form of the *Chi-Rho* symbol (XP, the first two letters of the word Christ in Greek).

The inscription itself is an intriguing one and has yet to be fully agreed on. The name *QONFAL* appears, followed by what seems to be an earlier inscription that may be *FILIA GVENNCREST*. An interesting thought is that Qonfal may have been the same person as the Cunoval name on the Mên Scryfa *(Site 90)*; or perhaps he was the patron saint of Gulval. The inscription has been dated to the sixth or seventh century AD.

A second inscribed stone is built into the north wall and is inscribed: *URITIN FILI SN*. It dates from the seventh or eighth century.

90 The Mên Scryfa Inscribed Stone, Morvah.

NG 427353. *Marked as:* Mên Scryfa – standing stone.
Direction as for Mên-an-tol (Site 29), but continuing along track for a further 300yds (274m). The stone can then be seen in the middle of a small field on the left.

The Mên Scryfa (Cornish for: Stone of Writing) is a granite pillar 6ft (1.8m) tall, on the northern face of which is one of the most clearly-legible inscriptions of any Dark Age inscribed stone

Running vertically down the stone in two lines, it reads: *RIALOBRAN· CVNOVAL· FIL·*, the last word of which is now below ground level. These are Latinised forms of Celtic names. The first is *Ryalvran* (Royal Raven), which is pure Cornish. The second is older and comes from the British *Cuno-uallos* (Famous Leader), which in a Cornish form would appear as *Kenwal*. The inscription is of the fifth or sixth century AD, although the stone itself may well have been a Bronze Age menhir.

The legend of Ryalvran is very old and exists only in fragments, but what can be gleaned is this: an enemy from the east forcibly took the lands of Kenwal and made his camp at Kenwal's fortress of Lescudjack Castle *(Site 64)*. His family were exiled, but Ryalvran returned in a bid to regain his father's lands. A great battle was fought at Gûnajynyal (Gendhal Moor or Anguidal Downs), where the Mên Scryfa stands, which ended in a confrontation between Ryalvran and his unnamed foe. The duel lasted long, but Ryalvran the warrior was slain, and buried beneath the stone.

This tale has a ring of truth to it. The local hero is not the victor, he is killed by a man whose name is not even remembered. It is thought that Ryalvran is also remembered in legend as the giant Holiburn who dwelt on Carn Galva, the towering crags of which dominate the area of the Mên Scryfa. It was said that the full length of the stone, 8ft 4ins (2.5m), was the height of the dead warrior although it is more

likely that his height corresponded to that of the stone when erect and exposing the whole of the inscription. This would have been around 6ft 4ins (1.9m), so that the warrior would still have been a notably big man.

The two names, which include the words for 'royal' and 'leader', almost certainly point to these two people having been a chieftain and his son.

Early last century, a 'clown of the neighbourhood' dug beneath the stone, believing that he would find treasure. If he found anything is not recorded, but his action caused the stone to topple and it lay on its inscribed face for many years before being re-erected. It is said that this 'clown' suffered the usual supernatural punishment.

91 Nûn Careg Stone Cross, St. Buryan.

NG 433246. *Not marked.*
Beside B3315 100yds (91m) N of the Merry Maidens stone circle (Site 30).

The front of this fine, round-headed cross has a Latin cross with widening arms cut in relief within a faint bead. The lower limb of the cross continues down the shaft. At the intersection of the arms is a small incised cross.

The rear of the cross head bears a curious cross, part of which is cut in relief, the rest of it shown by an incised outline.

92 Old Lanyon Mediaeval Settlement, Madron.

NG 422338. *Not marked.*
Directions as for West Lanyon Quoit (Site 14). Site lies in W corner of same field.

Within a small, fenced-off enclosure are the remains of Old Lanyon, home of the Lanyon family from the twelfth century AD. The farmhouse, of 'longhouse' type, was at first a small building, measuring 24ft (7.3m) by 11ft (3.3m) internally, and with walls 5ft (1.5m) thick. It was replaced on the same site by a building 27ft (8.2m) long by 16ft (4.9m) wide, with walls 2½ft (0.7m) thick. It was divided by a cross-passage into a byre, drained through the west wall, and a

living room with a *talfat*, or platformed half-floor, at one end. This house was later extended a further 19ft (5.8m) eastwards and was separated by a paved path from a similar house to the north. The second house was demolished for a tiny cottage to be built on its site, probably in the eighteenth century.

After abandonment as dwellings in the early fourteenth century, these houses were used as farm buildings and an additional barn was built. The southern longhouse, the walls of which survive to a height of 3ft (0.9m), the barn, the eighteenth-century cottage and its outbuildings comprise the ruins visible today.

The site was excavated by the Cornwall Archaeological Society in 1964.

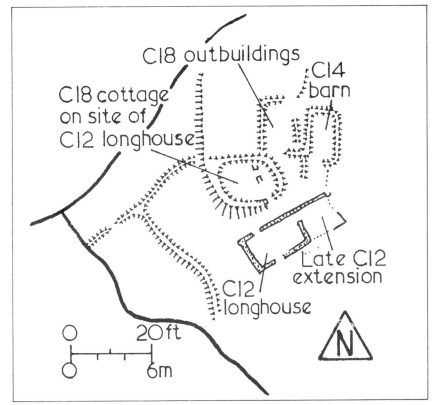

Penlee stone cross.

93 Penlee House Stone Cross, Penzance.

NG 471301. *Not marked.*
In forecourt of Penlee House Museum, Morrab Road, Penzance.

This massive, wheel-headed cross, some 8ft (2.4m) tall and now on a modern, stepped plinth, once stood in the Green Market in Penzance. From there it was moved to the corner of the Green Market and Causewayhead before being erected on its present site.

The front of the cross head has the outlines of four simple incised triangles forming a cross, while the back, possibly unfinished, has a Latin cross in relief, the lower limb of which was probably meant to extend down the shaft.

The front and sides of the tapered shaft have simple incised panels which alternately are blank and decorated by lines of small, shallow holes. The only exception is a side panel which shows a small, incised figure with a tail.

This cross is of great interest in that it is one of two in Cornwall to bear the inscribed name of a Cornish king. A scarcely legible inscription at the base of the shaft reads *REGIS RICATI CRUX* (the cross of King Ricatus), and is dated to between AD 900 and 930. It is possible that Ricatus was the predecessor, maybe the father, of King Howal, Cornwall's last recorded King.

94 Porth Chapel, Chapel and Holy Well, St. Levan.

NG 381219. *Marked as:* **well.**
Reached by footpath S from St. Levan church, or by cliff path W from Porthcurno.

The holy well of St. Selevan stands by the path on the clifftop above Porth Chapel beach. Three walls of large granite blocks stand to a height of 4ft (1.2m), while the floor, a vast slab of granite, covers the spring which flows out at the southern end. The water is still used for baptism at the church.

From the well, an ancient flight of about 50 stone steps descends to the tiny and scanty remains of the chapel which was built against the cliff on a ledge. It consisted of two rooms, the eastern of which was the chapel itself, measuring 12ft (3.7m) by 6ft (1.8m) internally. The western room was a cell, 9½ft (2.9m) long by 6ft (1.8m) wide, presumably the saint's living quarters. Both rooms were built on platforms cut into the cliff-face.

When excavated by Dr. V. Favell in 1931, fragments of thick, rough slating were found, and the chapel is believed to date from at least the eighth century, one of the oldest such chapels in Cornwall.

Plan of the Porth Chapel site (94)

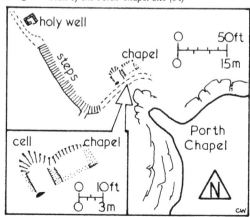

95 St. Just Plèn-an-Gwary, St. Just.

NG 370314. *Not marked.*
In the centre of St. Just, behind the prominent clock in Bank Square.

This is a rare example of a mediaeval amphitheatre, the only other existing example being St. Piran's Round near Perranporth. 126ft (38.4m) in diameter, it is encircled by a grassy bank still 6ft (1.8m) high. It has been extensively rebuilt in recent times and no trace now remains of the six rows of rough seats that were cut into the bank.

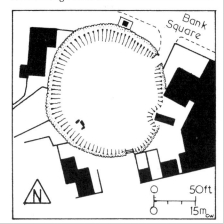

The mediaeval Cornish miracle plays, of which five manuscripts survive, were performed here and sports, including wrestling, were also held in the arena. The Wesleys used it to preach to thousands of tin miners and, in recent years, the Cornish Gorsedd has been held here. Stones pocked with deep drill holes from miners' competitions are still to be seen in the arena.

96 Sancreed Stone Crosses, Sancreed.

NG 420293. *Not marked.*
In churchyard.

The two tall crosses here are among the finest in Cornwall. One, by the south porch, is the work of the late ninth or early tenth century Cornish sculptor Runhol, whose signature *RUNHO* can be seen inscribed on a panel at the base of the cross. His other known work is the cross at Lanherne, Newquay, which originally stood at Roseworthy between Hayle and Camborne. On that cross, he signed himself *RUHOL*.

On the front of his elaborate Sancreed cross is a Christ figure with halo, set within the beaded limbs of the cross head, the back of which has a central boss surrounded by a fine knotwork design. Both front and back of the tall shaft are covered in beautiful double knotwork. One side has an incised geometric design, the other has carved serpentine knotwork. The head of this cross once stood on the churchyard wall before its shaft was found built into a wall inside the church.

The second cross, 9ft (2.7m) tall, also bears an inscription at the foot of its shaft, the letters *INCX X* being visible. The head of this cross is similar to that of its neighbour and all four sides of the shaft have incised designs. One of these, on a panel taking up most of the front of the shaft, shows a vase holding a long-stemmed flower, the head of which resembles a simple fleur-de-lis. It is possible that this cross is also the work of Runhol.

97 The Selus Stone, Inscribed Stone, St. Just.

NG 372315. *Not marked.*
In N aisle of St. Just church.

The face of this stone, which is 5½ft (1.6m) high and stands on a modern plinth, is engraved with a late form of the *Chi-Rho* monogram, surrounded by a simple incised border which extends down the length of the stone.

Another side of the pillar is inscribed with the words *SELVS IC IACIT*: 'Selus lies here'. Above the word 'Selus' are two characters which are probably the letters *NI*. Some think that these are part of the name, making it Senilus, Senlius or Selnius, but they appear to be later than the main inscription.

Possibly they were carved by a local wit to represent a Cornish negative, as if to change the inscription to 'Selus does not lie here'.

The stone was found when the chancel was pulled down prior to rebuilding in 1834. There is a report that, when the stone was being set up in its present position, a local man saw the word *PRESBYTER* (priest) carved at the bottom end of the pillar.

Bearing this in mind, it is possible that Selus was Selyv, or Selyf, brother of the Justin who became St. Just. These two are named as sons of Gerent and Enid, and Selyv was probably Selevan (now St. Levan).

The inscriptions on the Selus Stone date from the fifth or sixth century AD.

98 Tremethick Stone Cross, Penzance.

NG 448302. *Marked as:* **cross.**
At junction of A3071 and lane to Tregavara 1 mile W of Penzance.

5½ft (1.6m) tall, this cross rises dramatically from the corner of a hedge and, in fact, stands on the remains of a Bronze Age round barrow. Shaped in the form of a Latin cross with stubby cross-arms, it formerly stood at Rose-an-beagle near Paul.

When caught in the beam of headlights, this cross resembles a grey ghost and has given a number of people a scare!

Selus stone

99 Vellansaga Stone Cross, St. Buryan.

NG 425259. *Marked as:* **cross.**
Beside St. Buryan – Lamorna lane 1¼ miles E of St. Buryan.

Standing outside a cottage and overshadowed by trees, this fine little example has an incised Latin cross on both faces of its round head, the lower limbs continuing down the full length of the shaft which is set into a rough granite base.

Right: *Vellansaga Stone Cross (99)*

100 Whitecross, Stone Cross, Whitecross.

NG 525344. *Not marked.*
In a prominent position beside A30 at Whitecross, halfway between Penzance and Hayle.

The hamlet takes its name from this cross which is kept perpetually white-washed. The circular head has a cross in relief within a wide bead on the side facing the road, while the other side has a Christ figure with outstretching arms, also within a bead. The figure's legs are cut off almost where they meet the body, perhaps a sign that they extended down the original shaft, now lost. The head of the figure leans to one side.
  The cross-head is now mounted on two blocks of stone, also whitewashed, which form a stepped plinth.

Left: *The stone cross at Whitecross (100)*

The Land's End Saints

The obscure Cornish saints are a mystery to most people. Little record survives from the time in which they lived, and where information does exist, it comes from documents and records written at a much later date. Some are remembered only in tradition and legend and, sadly, nothing at all is known about a number of these early Celtic priests.

A number of saintly names appear in one form or another in the Land's End district and the following list may help to give a little insight into the identities of these holy men and women of the fifth, sixth and seventh centuries.

ST. ANTA Little is known of this presumably female saint, who may have founded the church or monastery of Lelant, originally *Lan Anta*. On the coast to the north of the church was the former site of Chapel Anja, probably a corruption of Anta.

ST. BERIANA The patron of St. Buryan, according to the Exeter Martyrology written five centuries later, was an Irish girl whose prayers apparently cured one of St. (King) Gerent's sons of paralysis.

ST. BRIGIT Morvah church is dedicated, not to a Celtic saint, but to the Swedish saint who founded the Bridgettine Order of Nuns during the fourteenth century. This Order once occupied St. Michael's Mount and Morvah is the only church in Britain dedicated to St. Brigit.

ST. CLEMENT The little island off Mousehole is named after the Bishop of Rome who was drowned in AD 99. Many sea-girt chapels like the one which formerly stood on this islet were dedicated to Clement who is also the patron saint of Trinity House.

ST. EUNY (UNY) Although little is known about him, Euny seems to have been quite an influential figure. Chapel Euny near Sancreed bears his hame and he is also a patron of Lelant (properly *Uny Lelant*), Crowan, Redruth, and a former church which existed at Merther Uny near Wendron. Mediaeval tradition declared him to be a brother of St. Ia and St. Erc (Erth).

ST. GWELVELA The identity of the name-saint of Gulval is a puzzle. At first glance it appears that the saint was a woman, but some believe that St. Gudwal, an early Breton bishop, may have settled here. There is a possibility that the Qonfal of the Madron church inscribed stone or the Cunoval of the Mên Scryfa (one and the same?) may have been the mysterious patron of Gulval.

ST. IA Pronounced 'eea', this saint was an Irish girl who sailed to St. Ives Bay with a number of other Irish saints. After her arrival, a local lord or chieftain named Dinan built a chapel for her at Porth Ia, now St. Ives. Legend states that she sailed over the Celtic Sea on a large leaf (a coracle?).

ST. JUST The name of St. Just graces two Cornish parishes, the other being on the Roseland peninsula near St. Mawes. He appears to have been Yestin, or Justin, a son of the Cornish king St. Gerent (probably not the Gerontius Rex of the early eighth century) who gave his name to the Roseland parish of Gerrans.

During the fifteenth century it was claimed that St. Just's relics still lay within his Penwith church where he was celebrated as a martyr. In Old Cornish, his name was pronounced 'east' and Priest's Cove, just beneath the nearby Cape Cornwall, is an abbreviation of Porth Just: St. Just's cove, pronounced 'Per' east.

ST. LEVAN St. Levan is a shortened form of Selevan, quite possibly the Selyf who was also a son of King Gerent. It has been suggested that the Selus of the inscribed stone in St. Just church may have been St. Just's brother Selyf, and it is worth noting that the word 'presbyter' (priest) was reportedly seen at the base of this stone. St. Selevan was said to have been the father of St. Cuby and lived his later life as a hermit at Porth Chapel, just below St. Levan church. There are several legendary anecdotes about him.

ST. LOY The remains of a tiny chapel dedicated to St. Loy or Elidius once stood on the cliff edge south of Boskenna House, but were destroyed last century. Also celebrated in the Isles of Scilly, Elidius was probably a seventh century bishop of Noyon, France.

ST. LUDEVAN It is thought that a saint of this name may have given his name to the parish of Ludgvan, but nothing more is known. Ludgvan church is dedicated to St. John.

ST. MADERN The identity of the saint who gave his name to Madron is difficult to ascertain. That he was Mactronus, disciple of the Welsh St. Tudwal, is more likely than the possiblity that he was the Irish St. Madarn or the Welsh St. Padarn, but none of these suggestions has any certain basis.

ST. PAUL The parish of Paul is named after the bishop St. Paul Aurelian, or Pol de Leon, who was a pupil of the Welsh St. Illtud. He later settled in Brittany where he founded the see of Leon, but on his journey from Wales visited his sister Sitafolla 'on the shores of the British Sea', possibly here at Mount's Bay. (This evidence was taken from a *Life of St. Paul Aurelian*, written in Brittany in AD 884 and based on a still earlier work.)

ST. SANCRED Mediaeval tradition declared that the saint of Sancreed lived as a swineherd as a penance for accidentally killing his father.

ST. SENAN There are problems of gender with the patron of Sennen. Pre-Reformation records suggest that the saint was a woman, St. Senana, but it is widely held that the Irish abbot Senan of Scattery Island, who died around AD 560, is the saint of the Land's End parish.

ST. SENARA Zennor is named after this obscure saint, but nothing at all is known about her.

ST. TEWENNOC Tewennoc, from whom Towednack takes its name, is a variant form of Winwallo, founder of the monastery of Landevennec in Cornouaille, Brittany, Landewednack and Gunwalloe, both on the Lizard peninsula of Cornwall, also commemorate this saint.

Tracing the Trackways

No one can be sure just when Penwith's ancient trackways came into being. They were certainly in use during the Bronze Age, with the advent of tin production, and could well have been trading routes as far back as the neolithic period, to carry locally-made stone axes from their 'factories' to points of distribution.

The Penwith peninsula still retains extensive traces of a system of trackways based on two major routes. These are often referred to as the 'Old St. Ives Road', and the 'Old Land's End Road', and both began close to known neolithic axe-factories on the western cliffs. Of the two, the 'Old St. Ives Road', also called the 'Watershed Way', is the better preserved, with most of its path still in existence, but in both cases, the extremities are uncertain and have largely to be guessed at. The reason for this is quite simple: the ends of the trackways are on lower ground and have therefore suffered from agriculture and building, whereas the middle parts are on bleak, rough moorland.

Both of the major tracks have important archaeological sites close by, and much of their routes were used later on when the parish boundaries were marked out. The best example of this is on the 'Old St. Ives Road', where the southern boundary of Morvah and Zennor parishes follows the trackway faithfully for five miles. This track traverses West Penwith's finest and wildest upland scenery, as it keeps to the highest parts of the peninsula's granite spine, above the once thickly-wooded valleys. Both trackways led to ancient trading ports: St. Ives, the Hayle estuary and St. Michael's Mount, and linked up with land routes from the east. Certainly by the Middle Ages, there were five such routes into the Land's End peninsula. Two of these were across fords; one across the mouth of the Marazion River (or River Lyd, to give its older name), the other crossing the dangerous low water flats of the Hayle estuary, from Carnsew, where there was an Iron Age fort, to Lelant. Just inland from each of these were routes across bridges; the Trevelyan bridge over the Lyd, and St. Erth bridge, probably the busiest route in mediaeval times, across the Hayle River. Both of these probably originated as fords. Finally, much of a dry route still exists across the higher land between the two rivers, leading from near Rosudgeon and entering the Penwith peninsula at Canon's Town.

Remains of many minor and tributary trackways can still be found throughout West Penwith but, as these are numerous and often fragmentary, it is best to concentrate on the two main ones: the Old St. Ives Road and the Old Land's End Road.

The Old St. Ives Road (The Tinners' Way)

To travel this route, either on foot or on horseback, is without doubt the finest way of seeing the spectacular and lonely Land's End moors. The track probably began close to the Kenidjack cliff castle *(Site 61)*, where there was a neolithic axe-factory, and near where tin and copper were almost certainly mined during the Bronze Age. It is worth noting that the cove of Porthledden, where the tin-rich Kenidjack valley opens to the sea, was guarded by two cliff castles: Kenidjack to the north and the destroyed trivallate site on Cape Cornwall to the south. No other cove in the Land's End peninsula was so heavily guarded, and it must, therefore, have been of great importance to the native population.

The best place to pick up the track is just off the B3306, in No Go By Lane at NG 374328, where an old rough lane (Water Lane) leads east, passing the scanty remains of a hut circle and associated pound in a field on its north side before opening onto the moorland expanse of Carnyorth Common, where it becomes a footpath. The Tregeseal stone circle *(Site 35)* is visible to the south-east, with several large round barrows between it and the prominent tor of Carn Kenidjack.

The path now swings north-east, climbing the hill over the remains of an extensive field system, and passing to the west of the legend-enshrouded Carn Kenidjack. The Kenidjack Common holed stones *(Site 26)*, not visible from the track, lie some 300 yards (270m) south-east of the Carn.

Leaving the moor, the path becomes an overgrown lane between fields to the north of the Carn, halfway along which is a cross-junction. Here, just down the southern branch, is the Boslow inscribed stone *(Site 79)* and the northern branch passes the Portheras Common round barrow *(Site 32)*. The route of the ancient trackway continues east, crossing the B3318 and becoming a well-used track skirting the southern edge of Woon Gumpus,

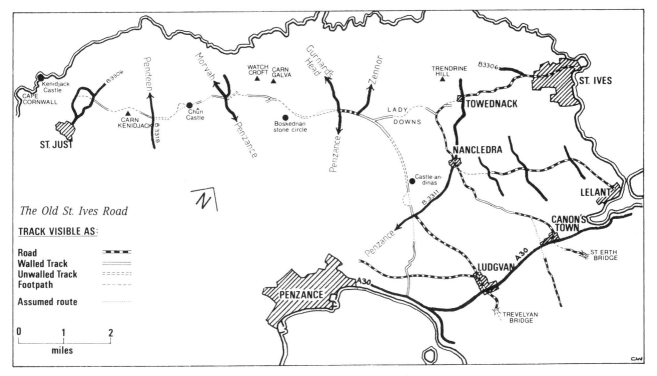

The Old St. Ives Road

TRACK VISIBLE AS:

Road	
Walled Track	
Unwalled Track	
Footpath	
Assumed route	

0   1   2
miles

famous in legend as the ghost- and sprite-haunted Gump. On the hillside above the track, like a silent sentinel, is the Boswens menhir *(Site 20)*.

At NG 401333, the route of the old track leaves the modern one, and is traceable as a path which then deviates slightly from the original line to approach Chûn Quoit *(Site 5)*, which has been in sight for some time. It then climbs to the hilltop and Chûn Castle *(Site 54)*, which was built astride the trackway.

On the north-east side of the castle, a faint path leads downhill beside an overgrown and stony depression marking where the trackway existed as a partially sunken way. Old reports of this part having been paved are probably due to the flattish appearance of natural outcrops which barely protrude above the ground.

At NG 407341, the path again becomes a narrow, scarcely-used lane between modern fields. At the bottom of this lane, and adjoining its southern side, is the superb courtyard house village of Bosullow Trehyllys *(Site 46)*.

Modern fields have all but obliterated the next 200 yards (180m) of the track, but a continuous stone hedge shows where it ran. On Carn Downs, close to the remains of more huts, fields and an unfinished round, it reappears as an unused lane bordered by low walls before opening onto the Morvah – Penzance road at NG 415347.

On the opposite side of the road is the long driveway to the Garden Mine Cottage, high on Watch Croft, and a path on the line of the old trackway leaves this at NG 418350, heading east and becoming a wide, overgrown lane bounded by stone walls. To the north is the summit of Watch Croft, at 826 feet (252m) the highest point in West Penwith, with its stone barrows and menhir *(Site 40)*, which are visible on the skyline. Just to the south of the track at this point are two groups of hut circles.

Some 200 yards (180m) after passing a parish boundary stone, the Mên Scryfa *(Site 90)* can be seen rising from the middle of a small field on the south side of the track, which is then joined by the well-worn lane from the Morvah – Penzance road and which passes the Mên-an-tol (Site 29). The next stretch of lane beyond this junction often tends to be wet before it opens onto moorland again. At this point is a large natural boulder called the Four Parishes Stone, its surface marked with a simple cross (marred by a modern drill-hole). This marks the exact meeting point of the ecclesiastical parishes of Morvah, Zennor, Gulval and Madron.

Up the boulder-strewn ridge to the south-east is the Boskednan stone circle (Site 19), with its attendant cemetery of round barrows. The huge, abrupt and jagged crag to the north is the 800ft (244m) southern peak of Carn Galva (spelt Galver, wrongly, on the maps).

The trackway now becomes a rather unclear footpath heading east, with a stone hedge on its northern side, and is marked by a number of parish boundary stones. On its eastern descent from the ridge, it becomes obscure, but a modern track leads down to the foot of the valley, crossing a rough lane at NG 444353.

On the opposite side of the lane is a footpath which climbs gradually, and passes close to the northern side of the Bodrifty hut settlement (Site 42) before striking out across the lonely expanse of moorland between Treen Beacon to the north, with its curious stone circle (Site 34) and round barrows, and Mulfra Hill, topped by its quoit (Site 7), to the south. (Mulfra Quoit cannot be seen from this part of the trackway.)

It is possible that the original trackway lay just a little to the north of this path, judging by the position of the parish boundary, of which three or four mark-stones can be found.

At the Gurnard's Head – Penzance road, met by the trackway at NG 452361, path and parish boundary converge once more and continue east along the Zennor turn-off, straight on down a rough lane to a fork at NG 464363, a place which bears the strange name of Bishop's Head and Foot. A stone cross which once stood here was lost for many years before Peter Pool and Vivien Russell found a worked Gothic cross-shaft nearby. Unhappily, this too has now vanished.

This fork preserves a branch in the original prehistoric track, and the right hand path heads off to the south-east, past a number of round barrows centred at NG 470360, then passing close to the western side of the Castle-an-dinas hill fort (Site 53). South of the fort, it now has to detour around the spoil-heaps of the huge roadstone quarry, then becomes a wide, grassy track which meets the B3311 at Castle Gate (NG 489341). From there its path is unclear, but it may have followed the line of a continuous hedge

from NG 488340 to 493332. From then on, lengths of used and disused lane bring it to the coast at Long Rock, close to the prehistoric trading port of Iktis (St. Michael's Mount).

Back at Bishop's Head and Foot, the left fork of the track continues north-east, along a stony lane before venturing onto the wide, flat expanse of Lady Downs. Here, the sharp-eyed can pick out Zennor Quoit (Site 15), ½ mile to the north-west. The track then turns further to the north, passing about 100 yards (90m) to the west of a large ring barrow at NG 475371. At 780 feet (238m), this is the highest point of the track. Lady and Amalveor Downs retain vestiges of an extensive system of trackways, one of which passes right by the north side of Zennor Quoit, to join another leading from the main trackway to the hut settlement of Sperris Croft (Site 71).

The main trackway now swings east, descending the hill as a walled, sunken path. Just to the north, at NG 479377, a Bronze Age gold hoard was found concealed in an ancient stone hedge in 1931. Now in the British Museum (replicas can be seen in the County Museum, Truro), this was probably the stock of a travelling Irish goldsmith.

At the foot of the hill, at Embla Vean Farm, the track branches once again. The northern fork is the easier to follow, continuing along the lane through Amalveor Farm, then appearing at NG 483378 as a footpath passing Towednack church. From there, the track is represented by the road to St. Ives turning off just north of the vicarage, past Breja Farm, skirting the south side of Rosewall Hill, and passing Higher Bussow, where there are hut circles and a mediaeval culverhouse. It then joins the B3306, leading down through Stennack into modern St. Ives.

The former existence of an Iron Age cliff castle on the Island may well indicate that a maritime settlement existed at St. Ives in prehistoric times, and, in later years, the Irish St. Ia is said to have landed here, perhaps a pointer to the probability that prehistoric and Dark Age St. Ives was commercially linked with Ireland.

The south-eastern fork of the track at Embla Vean connected with another, and possibly even more important, trading port on the Hayle estuary, close to Lelant. The exact route is difficult to trace and these last notes are largely guesswork.

It may have followed the path of the present lane as far as Nancledra, then continued on the line of a footpath which winds its way east from the council houses (keep to southern fork at NG 499361). At NG 504362 it crosses a lane, beside which, 100 yards

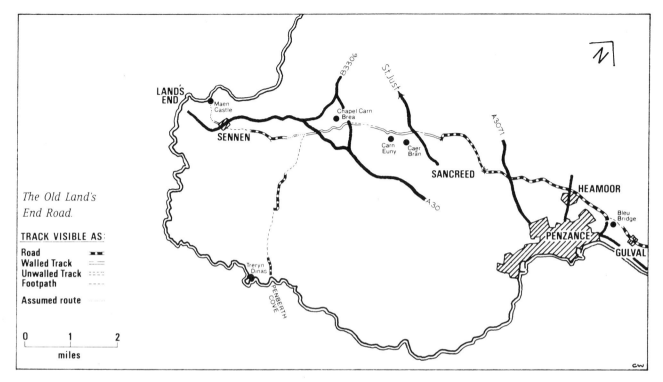

The Old Land's
End Road.

TRACK VISIBLE AS:

Road
Walled Track
Unwalled Track
Footpath

Assumed route

0   1   2

miles

(90m) to the south, stands the Brunnion Carn cross *(Site 80)*.

As it continues east, the path crosses another lane and finally comes out at NG 509364, on the Lelant Downs – Cripple's Ease road, just south of Brunnion Farm.

The rocky hill to the east is Trencrom, with its spectacularly-sited hill fort *(Site 72)* and, to the north-west is the flat-topped Trink Hill, crowned by a ruinous ring barrow. On the southern slopes of the hill are the battered remnants of a courtyard house village, faint, fragmented, and difficult to find among the remains of the defunct Wheal Reeth mine.

The path of the trackway may be the road leading to Trevarrack, with the Beersheba menhir *(Site 16)* to the south-east, and thence to the A3074 at Higher Trenoweth (NG 533380). Opposite is the lane to Lelant church, the final part of the trackway route to the Hayle estuary.

Yet another branch of the trackway occurs at Nancledra, and is represented by the lane leading south-east from the village to

Lock Farm. Just east of the farm, at NG 504355, a bridleway leads all the way to Canon's Town. Here, it branches again; one way leading east towards St. Erth bridge, the other, south-east towards Rosudgeon.

The Old Land's End Road *(Vounder Gogglas)*

This track really survives only in the middle of its course and much of the remainder has to be guessed at. It probably entered the peninsula either at the mouth of the Lyd, or at Trevelyan bridge, and made its way west to the present site of Gulval. Dipping into Barlowena Bottoms and passing the Bleu Bridge inscribed stone *(Site 76)*, its westward course may well be the present road from the B3311 to Heamoor. An alternative route could have run along the Eastern Green, now followed by the A30, turning inland at Chyandour to the junction of the B3311 and the Heamoor road.

The present road from Heamoor to Tremethick Cross, overlooked by the Lesingey Round hill fort *(Site 65)*, may be close to the trackway route. Crossing the A3071 ¼ mile north-west of the Tremethick stone cross *(Site 98)*, a lane continues westwards, crossing a stream at NG 434302, then forking. The right (north) fork is on the known trackway route, at first leading north-west, then swinging round in a wide curve to head south-west, meeting another stream at NG 415300, just below Enestreven Farm.

So far, the route has passed through farmland, and been replaced by modern roads, but now it begins to meet moorland and emerges in something like its original form. From the stream, it becomes a rough track climbing steeply on the western side of Sancreed Beacon, on the summit of which is a pair of large round barrows. An enclosed hut settlement also exists on the north-western flank of the hill.

The track degenerates into a mere footpath before crossing the St. Just – Sancreed road at NG 410295. It is then clearly visible as a stony, waterworn track continuing south-west and uphill. At the brow of the ridge, it passes within 200 yards (180m) of the Caer Brân hill fort *(Site 48)*, the tall rampart of which can be seen clearly to the south-east. The fort is approached from the trackway by an overgrown lane between two very low stone and turf walls. The age of this lane is unknown, but is likely to be very old indeed.

The main trackway now descends the southern slope and meets a T-junction. The southern (left) branch should be taken. At NG 401289 it passes within 100 yards (90m) of the Carn Euny courtyard house village and fogou *(Site 50)*, then swings back in a westerly direction, passing the holy well of Chapel Euny *(Site 82)*, which lies right beside the path.

The track now heads south-west in a straight line along the southern foot of Bartinney Hill, capped by the enigmatic earthwork of Bartinnê Castle *(Site 41)*, and passing beneath a disused china-clay quarry. It then crosses the road linking the A30 and B3306 – the stone cross of Crows-an-wra *(Site 84)* stands ½ mile to the south-east – and becomes a rather overgrown, walled track passing across the southern flank of Britain's first and last hill, Chapel Carn Brea. This hill, topped by its huge stone barrow *(Site 4)*, is said to have the widest sea-horizon of any mainland viewpoint in the country.

The trackway crosses the A30 at Newshop, but peters out on Trevorrian Common at NG 380271. It is believed that a branch of the track from this point led to Penberth Cove, and a continuous route of footpath and lane still exists, leading south-east through the farms of Bosanketh and Bosfrankan, the hamlet of Crean, and down the Penberth valley to the sea.

The main track, which, incidentally, is called locally 'Grassy Lane' along its course between Caer Brân and Newshop, reappears briefly at NG 378268. Its route is next picked up as the lane through Trevear Farm, heading west towards the A30 at Escalls Green. Before it reaches the main road, however, the trackway leaves the lane, and leads south-west as the pathway to Sennen church.

On the west side of the A30, just south of the church, a fragmentary track leads out onto the open Treve Common (note a menhir standing in a hedge just to the north), from which a path may have followed the stream north-west to the Iron Age Maen Cliff Castle *(Site 67)*, the end of the road, within sight of the End of the Land.

Land's End Place-Names

It is obvious to anyone visiting Cornwall that the majority of its place-names are not of the English tongue. Anglo-Saxon names, which predominate throughout England, vanish almost without trace west of the River Tamar. The change is dramatic, but not really surprising in view of Cornwall's history. Cornish place-names, which to the 'foreigner' are strange to look at and stranger to pronounce, derive from the Cornish language.

The Cornish language deserves a mention in this book: after all, it is a 'living' ancient monument and, before recent efforts to revive it, the Land's End peninsula was its last outpost.

Kernewek, to give its proper name, is, as has been mentioned earlier, a descendant of the Brythonic or British language spoken by the Celts of Brittany and mainland Britain throughout the Iron Age and Romano-British times. Like all languages, it changed with time and, as the Anglo-Saxon advance effectively cut off the Celts of Wales and Cornwall from each other, so the language was affected, becoming separate dialects, then separate languages. Similarly, the language of the Breton Celts also began to differ. Irish Gaelic influences in large parts of Wales altered the language there even further until there were three distinct tongues: Cornish, Welsh and Breton, the latter being more closely akin to Cornish than is Welsh.

It was during mediaeval times that Cornish began to falter as a mother tongue, its use being pushed further and further west by political pressure from England until, by the beginning of the eighteenth century, it was confined to the Land's End and Lizard peninsulas. It is often stated that Dorothy (Dolly) Pentreath of Mousehole (died 1777) was the last person to speak Cornish as a mother tongue but, in fact, native speakers persisted into the nineteenth century. The language never really died, and is now enjoying a considerable revival both at evening class and in a number of homes.

Many Cornish place-names are now almost impossible to decipher. They have been misspelt and respelt over the years and are subject to the peculiar English habit of altering a strange word to look like a more familiar one. An example of this is the 'Lizard'. Who would have thought that this was once a Cornish name: *Lys arth* (stronghold in a high place)! Even worse, the startling 'Skidnywidny' is a grotesque corruption of *Skyber wyn* (white barn). Nevertheless, the pastime of translating Cornish place-names is a fascinating one.

Nouns commonly found in Cornish names are:

BAL: a digging or mine.

BOS: dwelling, home. This sometimes appears as *bo, bod, bot* or *boj*, and is often followed by a personal name, e.g. Bosliven (home of Selevan).

BRE: hill. Pronounced 'bray', this mainly appears as *brea* (same pronunciation).

CAR, KER: fort or defensive enclosure. It is often seen as Caer and Gear. The plural form, *kerrow*, is also found as a place name.

CARN: a large rock outcrop; when on a hilltop it is the same as a Devonian tor. It may also refer to an ancient stone barrow. This word is still readily understood by Cornish people, and is in everyday use.

CARREK: rock. It is often corrupted to *carrick, garrick* or *garrack*.

CHY: house (pronounced 'chee'). In some names it may be spelt *jy, gy, ty,* or, at the end of a word, *-sy*. Unfortunately, it is now usually pronounced to rhyme with 'cry'.

CROWS: a cross (rhymes with 'cows'). Often corrupted to *grouse*.

DOWR: water. This rhymes with 'cower', and is found as *dower* and *dour*.

DYNAS: fort, castle. Pronounced 'dinn-us'. This is often seen in place-names as *dinas, dennis* and *dinnis*.

EGLOS: a church.

ENYS: island, isolated place. This is often spelt *ennis*, and is sometimes found as *ninnis, ninnes (an enys)* – the island/isolated place.

GUN: downland. Pronounced 'goon' and often spelt that way. It will also be found as *woon* and *noon (an wun* – the downs).

GWEL: field. Pronounced 'gwail', and corrupted to *gweal* and *gul*.

HAL: wet or marshy moorland. This can be found as *hale*, and can be confused with *hayl*.

HAYL: estuary.

KELLY: copse or grove. Often spelt *killy, gilly* and *gelly*.

LAN: enclosure, usually a sacred one, so this can be loosely translated to mean 'church'. Many Celtic churches were, and sometimes still are, within a round or oval enclosure, often raised. Confusion can arise with *lyn*, e.g. Lanyon, which is derived from *lyn yeyn* – cold pool.

LOGH: pool. This is pronounced 'low', with the final 'h' being lightly breathed (the 'g' is silent). This can also mean 'haven' or 'anchorage' and is found as *loe* and *looe*.

LYN: also means a pool.

LYS: court, stronghold, chieftain's seat. Pronounced 'liz', it is usually found as *les* or *lis*.

MELYN: mill. As this often appears as *mellin, vellan* and *vellin*, it can be confused with *melen*, the Cornish for 'yellow'.

MEN: stone (pronounced 'main'). This can also be seen as *maen, ven, mayne*. The plural is *meyn* (pronounced 'mine'), appearing as *mine* and *vine*, and *meynek*, meaning stony, can be found as *minack*.

NANS: valley. Also spelt *nance* and *nant*.

PEN: head, end, top. It is often taken to mean 'headland' (properly *Pentyr*) in most coastal place-names. It is also found with the spelling *pedn*, this deriving from late Cornish pronunciation which, after a short vowel, tended to add a 'd' before a final 'n', and 'b' before 'm'.

POL: pool, creek, pit.

PONS: bridge. Often corrupted to *ponds* and *pont*.

PORTH: cove, especially one where boats can land. In inland names it means 'gate' or 'entrance'. It is often shortened to *por, par, per* or *pr'*.

ROS: heathland or, sometimes, a promontory larger than an ordinary headland. This word is usually found as *rose*, but some confusion with *res* (ford) can arise.

SAUN: a chasm in a coastal cliff. Usually found as *zawn*.

TOWAN: sand-dune. With the first syllable rhyming with 'now', this is another word which is still in common use.

TRE, TREF: tre, pronounced 'tray', originally meant a farm, but can now be applied to any community from a farm to a town. At the end of names it is often mutated to *dra* or *drea* and, at the beginning of a word, may just appear as *tr'*.

WHEL: a mine (literally, work). Pronounced 'whale' and found in place-names as *wheal* and *huel*.

Some adjectives which are also common in Cornish place-names are:

BRAS: great. This rhymes with 'shares', and often appears as *braze, vraze* and *brawze*.

BYGHAN: small. This is pronounced 'bee-an', with a lightly breathed 'h' between the syllables. This word is almost always found as *bean* or *vean* in place-names, and even these should be pronounced as two syllables, not 'been' or 'veen'.

COTH: old.

DU: black. Often spelt *dhu, sew* and *thew*.

GLAS: found as *glase* or *glaze*, this is a confusing one. It means 'green', 'grey' and 'blue'! *(gwer*, pronounced 'gwair', also means 'green').

GWYN: white or fair. Also found as *gwidden, quidden, widn, win*, etc.

HEN: old.

HYR: long. Pronounced 'here', it can appear as *heere*.

MELEN: yellow, but be careful of confusion with *melyn*, a mill.

MUR: great, large. Pronounced 'meer', it is usually found as *meor*, or *veor*.

NOWETH: new.

SEGH: dry. Pronounced 'say', it can appear as *seth, zeath, seg*, etc.

YEYN: cold, bleak. This rhymes with 'nine', and can be found as *jane, jean* and *yon*. Thus, *Chapel Jane* has nothing to do with any person of that name, but means 'bleak chapel'.

Pronunciation is not always what might be expected, and it invariably catches out the non-Cornishman. For example, it is usual for an Englishman to stress the first syllable of a word, but not so in Cornish. In two-syllable words, the second is usually stressed, as in Pen**zance**, while in longer words, the stress is on the penultimate syllable, e.g. Tre**sid**der. The town of Liskeard in East Cornwall has a name that will catch out any stranger. It is not **Lis**keerd, but Lis**kard**.

Just to confuse matters a little more, the initial letters of some Cornish nouns mutate under certain conditions: 'g' may change to 'w' (*gun* – downs; *an wun* – the downs); 'b' to 'v' or f; 'gw' to 'w' or 'qu'; 'p' to 'b'; 't' to 'd'; 'm' to 'v'; 'k' to 'g'; 'c' to 'g'; 'ch' to 'j'; 'd' to 'th'; and an initial 'g' may vanish completely (*Gunlas* – green downs, from *gun glas*).

These problems occur regularly in the place-names of the Land's End peninsula, so here is a small selection with their pronunciation, meaning and original form:

BOLEIGH (bo**lay**) – dwelling by a ?stone slab? (*bos legh*).

BOSCAWEN-UN (boscaw**noon**) – dwelling by an elder tree on the downs (*bos scawen an wun*).

BOSPORTHENNIS (bos**pren**is) – dwelling at the entrance to an isolated spot (*bos porth enys*).

BOTREA (bo**tray**) – ?farm dwelling? (*bos tre*).

CAER BRAN (care brain) – Fort Crow (*ker bran*).

CARN BREA (carn bray) – tor, or stone barrow, on a hill (*carn bre*).

CARN GLOOSE (carn glooz) – grey rock (*carrek las*).

CHUN (choon) – house on the downs (*chy wun*).

CROWS-AN-WRA (crows – to rhyme with 'cows' – an ray) – the witch's cross (*crows an wragh*).

GUN RITH (goon reeth) – red downs (*gun ruth*).

KENIDJACK ken**idj**ek) – hooting tor (*carn ujek*).

LESCUDJACK (les**cud**jek) – shielded stronghold (*lys scosek*) or wooded stronghold (*lys cosek*).

MEN SCRYFA (main **scrifa**) – stone of writing (*men scryfa*).

NANJISAL (nan**jizza**l) – low valley (*nans ysel*).

PENNANCE (p'**nance**) – end of the valley (*pen nans*).

PENWITH (pen**with**) – furthest end (*penwyth*).

TREASSOWE (**trazz**a) – *tre*(farm) + ?

TREGESEAL (trege**zeel**) – *tre*(farm) + ? + ?*hal*? (wet moor).

TREREIFE (treev) – *tre*(farm) + ?

TRERYN (treen) – promontory farm/village *(tre ryn)*.

TREVEAL (tre**vail**) – Beli's farm.

TREWERN (**traw**en) – farm by a marsh *(tre gwern)*

TREWOOFE (trove) – Smith's farm *(tre gof)*.

A selection of books and booklets about Cornish place-names can be found in bookshops throughout Cornwall, but a number of these are misleading or give misinformation. By far the best are by people who really know the Cornish tongue. Three works are strongly recommended: *The Place Names of West Penwith* by Peter Pool (the Bard Gwas Galva); *A Popular Dictionary of Cornish Place-Names* by O.J. Padel, and *A Guide to Cornish Place Names* by the late R. Morton Nance (Mordon).

Bibliography

WEST PENWITH

Cooke, I., *Journey to the Stones*, Men-an-Tol Studio, 1987.

Maxwell, I.S., *Historical Atlas of West Penwith*, University of Sheffield, Department of Geography, 1976.

Michell, J., *The Old Stones of Land's End*, Garnstone Press, 1974; Pentacle Books, 1979.

Pool, P.A.S., *The Place Names of West Penwith*, Federation of Old Cornwall Societies, 1973.

Pool, P.A.S., and King, M., *Antiquities of Penwith*, Penwith District Council, 1979.

Rowe, L., *Granite Crosses of West Cornwall*, D. Bradford Barton, 1973.

Russell, V., *West Penwith Survey*, Cornwall Archaeological Society, 1971.

Thomas, A.C., Pool, P.A.S., Weatherhill, C., *The Principal Antiquities of the Land's End District*, Cornwall Archaeological Society, 16th edn. 1980.

CORNWALL AND THE SOUTH WEST

Barnett, J., *Prehistoric Cornwall: The Ceremonial Sites*, Turnstone Press, 1982.

Borlase, W., *Antiquities Historical and Monumental of the County of Cornwall, 1754*, EP Publishing, 1973.

Clark, E., *Cornish Fogous*, Methuen, 1961.

Fox, A., *South West England*, David and Charles, 1973.

Grinsell, L., *Discovering Regional Archaeology: South West England*, Shire, 1970.

Halliday, F.E., *A History of Cornwall*, Duckworth, 2nd edn. 1975.

Langdon, A.G., *Old Cornish Crosses*, Truro, 1896.

Nance, M., *A Guide to Cornish Place Names*, Federation of Old Cornwall Societies, 1963.

Padel, O.J., *A Popular Dictionary of Cornish Place-Names*, Alison Hodge, 1988.

Pearce, S., *The Archaeology of the South West*, Collins, 1981.

Pearce, S., *The Kingdom of Dumnonia*, Lodenek Press, 1978.

Pevsner, N., *The Buildings of England: Cornwall*, Penguin, 2nd edn. 1970.

Vulliamy, C.E., *Prehistoric Remains in West Penwith*, Lanham, St. Ives, 1921.

Weatherhill, C., *Cornovia: Ancient Sites of Cornwall and Scilly*, Alison Hodge, 1985.

Woolf, C., *Introduction to the Archaeology of Cornwall*, D. Bradford Barton, 1970.

Cornish Archaeology, annual journal of the Cornwall Archaeological Society.

GENERAL ARCHAEOLOGICAL BOOKS WHICH INCLUDE SITES IN WEST PENWITH

Bord, J., and C., *A Guide to Ancient Sites in Britain*, Latimer New Dimensions, 1978; Paladin, 1979.

Burl, A., *Prehistoric Stone Circles*, Shire, 1979.

Burl, A., *The Stone Circles of the British Isles*, Yale University Press, 1976.

Cunliffe, B., *Iron Age Communities in Britain*, Routledge and Kegan Paul, 1978.

Dyer, J., *Discovering Archaeology in England and Wales*, Shire, 1976.

Dyer, J., *Southern England: An Archaeological Guide*, Faber 1973.

Laing, L., *The Archaeology of late Celtic Britain and Ireland*, Methuen, 1975.

Laing, L., *Celtic Britain*, Routledge and Kegan Paul, 1979.

Laing, L., and J., *A Guide to the Dark Age Remains in Britain*, Constable, 1979.

Thomas, N., *Guide to Prehistoric England*, Batsford, 2nd edn. 1976.

Wainright, R., *A Guide to the Prehistoric Remains in Britain*, Constable, 1978.

LOCAL LORE AND LEGEND

Bottrell, W., *Traditions and Hearthside Stories of West Cornwall*, Vols. I–III, Bottrell, 1st series, 1870; Frank Graham, 1970.

Cook, J., *When I Set Out for Lyonesse ...Cornish Walks and Legends*, Alison Hodge, 1984.

Courtney, M.A., *Cornish Feasts and Folklore*, Beare, Penzance, 1890; E.P. Publishing, 1973.

Hunt, R., *Popular Romances of the West of England*, Chatto and Windus, 1923; Benjamin Blom, 1968.

Index of Sites